FOUR ROSES IN THREE ACTS

FOUR ROSES
in
THREE ACTS

by
Franklin Mason

FICTION COLLECTIVE, INC   NEW YORK

First Edition

Copyright © 1981 by Franklin Mason

Library of Congress Catalog No.: 80-68007
ISBN: 0-914590-64-2 (hardcover)
ISBN: 0-914590-65-0 (paperback)

Published by FICTION COLLECTIVE, INC.

The publication of this book is in part made possible with support from the National Endowment for the Arts, a Federal agency, and the New York State Council on the Arts; and with the cooperation of the Teachers and Writers Collaborative (New York).

Typeset at Open Studio in Rhinebeck, New York, a non-profit facility for writers, artists and independent publishers, funded in part by grants from the New York State Council on the Arts and the National Endowment for the Arts.

THIS BOOK IS FOR HEDDA

You may break, you may shatter the vase, if you will,
But the scent of the roses will hang round it still.

—Thomas Moore

ACT ONE

Up In Michigan

Ernest Hemingway liked it up in Michigan, liked it fine. It was always fine weather up in Michigan. Cold but fine. Cold enough to freeze a brass monkey. Some cold, eh?

"I like it fine," Ernest said.

Ernest was in Petoskey, sitting in Brown's Beanery. Drinking.

Ernest worked in a pump factory in Petoskey. Not women's shoes, but like if you have a flat tire and a bicycle and a pump, you could blow it up.

Ernest wasn't talking to anyone but himself. "I couldn't have a better audience," Ernest said.

There must have been many flat tires in Petoskey, considering all the pumps. But Ernest wasn't a flat tire. Or so he told himself.

There were Indians up in Michigan. "Ha-ha," they went. They laughed a lot.

Sometimes the laughter sounded like the old South. There weren't Indians in the old South but Sherwood Anderson was there. He heard the Negroes laugh in the old South.

It wasn't just pumps Ernest turned out. He turned out prose too. It was fine prose, hand wrought and hard wrought like the pumps.

3

After work Ernest would shovel his way out of the factory. He'd shovel to Brown's Beanery and write. Then shovel home and write. He was a writing man. What he shoveled was snow. It was all over the place.

Ernest kept a pet bird inside his shirt. Max Eastman said it was fake. They fought about it.

"I'll write about the Indians," Ernest said, still to himself. There wasn't anybody much you could talk to in Petoskey.

Ernest wrote about how the Indians went hunting and trapping, how they got drunk. Ernest went hunting and trapping and got drunk with them. His prose got finer and finer all the time. The weather got finer too.

The weather and the prose got too fine for Petoskey. For Ernest too. He walked out of the pump factory in the middle of the night. Into a snowstorm. Like Sherwood Anderson from his paint factory.

Ernest never went back. "Never look backwards," Ernest said. "You can't go to your house again." Ernest left and took his fine prose elsewhere.

Meanwhile In Paris

In Paris there was Gertrude Stein.

She hadn't always been there, she'd been at Radcliffe. She knew William James.

"You are all a lost generation," William told her. Gertrude wondered what she'd lost.

William knew how smart she was.

"I don't feel like taking a test," Gertrude said.

"That's all right," said William. He passed her anyhow. That's smart.

What Gertrude did in Paris was art. She did other things too. But she didn't go hunting and trapping in Paris. Or drinking. At least, as far as we know, she didn't go drinking. Art was it.

There were painters all over the place. Picasso, Braque, Juan Gris, you name him. Gertrude had him in tow or he had Gertrude in tow.

It was a great time in Paris and the weather always fine.

The weather of the Twenties was always fine, up in Michigan, up in Paris, up anywhere. Never in the history of the world had there been so much fine weather.

Sometimes there was a false spring but it didn't stay false

long. It got true. Then everybody was happy.

People came and went. It was a great time for coming and going. People stayed to tea and had little biscuits. There was talk, talk, talk, talk, talk.

And all this time Gertrude was writing her head off. She wrote and wrote and wrote and wrote and wrote. But they didn't print and print and print and print and print. Not even print once.

That's the way it is with writers. They work away and work away. Ernest worked away and worked away and so did Gertrude. But in another part of the world.

Would they ever meet, these two who worked away and worked away? That is the question.

Getting A Big Plum

Up in Michigan was not up enough for Ernest. He wanted it
upper and he packed his pen and went to Toronto. That is upper
than Michigan.

In Toronto Ernest got a job on this newspaper, the *Toronto
Star.*

Ernest hunted and trapped up in Toronto. He did some
drinking. There is always some drinking at newspapers. He did
some writing. There is always some writing at newspapers.

But newspaper writing did not fill Ernest's heart's desire. Ernest
also wrote his own writing, his own type of writing. Trying to fill his
heart's desire.

But Ernest did good newspaper writing too. Newspapers are
funny, they like you to do a good bit of their type of writing.

Ernest was coming up in the world. He was writing feature
stories. Writing feature stories is coming up in the newspaper
world.

Then one day the *Toronto Star* said, "Ernest, how about going
to Paris?"

Paris was not up like Michigan or Toronto but it was across

the water. Across the water was most certainly what Ernest wanted and especially Paris.

You could not have given him a bigger plum.

Ernest took the plum and ate it.

"Yes," Ernest said, "I will go to Paris."

But the world is never simple, only the people in it.

There were things Ernest had to do, had to do to get ready for Paris. Ernest had to pack four wives.

On the other side of the water there was Paris. And the Tuileries and the Louvre and the Luxembourg Gardens and the Left Bank and all the rest of it. And Gertrude Stein. But you already know that.

How do you like the way things are going so far?

Something About A Machine

Every once in the while and sometimes quite often, Gertrude Stein would go out in her machine. That's what they were called then, what automobiles were called. Now they are called cars and if anyone said machines today, you would say ha-ha.

Anyhow, Gertrude Stein did go out about the countryside. It was pleasant in those days to go out in the countryside, especially in a machine. It was pleasant to go out in the city too.

It was fine in Paris. And in the outskirts of Paris, it was fine too, fine as silk.

Maybe here you ought to know that Gertrude did not drive the machine. She could but she didn't.

Alice B. Toklas was the one who drove the machine. She drove Gertrude all about in the country and in the city too.

You have no doubt seen pictures of Gertrude Stein and Alice B. Toklas in their machine. They are pleasant pictures to see. Wasn't it fine of them, two women traveling about in their machine that way?

"Let's go for a drive," said Gertrude.

In those days if you had a machine, you went for a drive.

"Yes," said Alice, "let's go for a drive."

9

Automobiles were an adventure in those days. Everyone takes them for granted today, like cereal in the morning. But in those days it was quite an adventure and anything could happen and did.

Now you just take engines in those days. Engines would boil over all over the place. You had to pour water in them to quiet them down.

And tires. Tires were so funny in those days when you look back on them now.

Tires were always going flat. Then you would have to pump them up or change them.

Do you know something? Maybe you'd go on a trip in a machine, maybe twenty-four miles or so, and do you know what would happen? Nineteen flat tires. Nineteen.

Oh, if you are young, you don't believe it. But ask any old-timer, he will tell you. Nineteen.

Anyhow, it was very adventurous to go about in a machine in those days. You see there were not too many machines. Oh, nothing like today.

It was adventurous and picturesque especially when Gertrude Stein and Alice B. Toklas went about the countryside or about the city.

Especially when the city was Paris. Something to see. You can believe that. The city was something to see and so were Gertrude and Alice.

A Note From Sherwood

At the same time Ernest was leaving the pump factory, Sherwood Anderson was leaving the paint factory. You may remember that. But they didn't bump into one another.

Now Ernest was leaving the newspaper and he did bump into Sherwood.

"Sorry," said Ernest.

"Nothing to be sorry about," said Sherwood.

Sherwood just happened to be passing through Toronto. Sherwood used to do a lot of passing through.

After Ernest and Sherwood bumped, they got to talking. They were both writing folk, so the talk turned to writing.

"Are you writing well?" Sherwood asked.

"Yes, I'm writing well," Ernest answered. "Are you writing well?" Ernest asked.

"Yes, I'm writing well," Sherwood answered.

Ernest said he was thinking of going to Paris. He knew dern well he was going to Paris.

"I'm thinking of going to Paris," Ernest said.

"Oh boy," said Sherwood.

"Yeah," Ernest said.

11

"Tell you what," Sherwood said. "I'll give you a letter to Gertrude Stein."

Sherwood had been around quite a bit, you see.

"Oh boy," said Ernest, "a letter to Gertrude."

So right there, Sherwood whipped out pen and paper and wrote a letter to Gertrude Stein.

"This is Ernest Hemingway," Sherwood wrote and then he signed his name which was Sherwood Anderson.

"Gosh," said Ernest.

Then Sherwood whipped out an envelope and put the letter in it. It didn't need a stamp because Ernest was taking the letter right with him.

"Golly day, thanks," said Ernest. "How can I ever repay you?"

"Write a book about me sometime," Sherwood said. "How are your wives?"

"Finer than the four horsemen* at Notre Dame," Ernest told him.

Then Ernest and Sherwood parted. Ernest had to be on his way to Paris and Sherwood had to be on his way to wherever his way was.

---

*Stuhldreher, Miller, Crowley and Layden.

Accumulating Wives

Ernest had four wives which he somehow accumulated. Ernest went hunting and trapping and accumulated wives.

Ernest did not know exactly how this came about.

"Maybe they are the ones that hunt and trap," Ernest said. This was at a time when Ernest himself felt hunted and trapped.

Loading four wives on a boat was fraught with difficulties. There was the bunk arrangement. There was the sitting with the captain at meals arrangement. You can see the difficulties.

Really this is a trying scene. The boat had scarcely put to sea when what do you think Ernest had on his hands? Ernest had on his hands: four seasick wives.

Let us be as kind as possible to Ernest and his wives. And to ourselves. Let us look the other way.

In normal times each wife had her role. This one did this, this one did that, this one did this, this one did that. But certainly their condition at this time was not normal. It was difficult to tell the different roles. In fact, they were all playing the same role. Somewhere along the rail.

Ernest's role was always the same and it was not difficult to tell his role.

13

Ernest had four wives. Their names were: Hadley, Pauline, Martha, Mary.

They might have had other names. Ernest might have called them other names.

Ernest called Marlene Dietrich the Kraut.

They were all on the boat together now. All in the same boat. Ernest and his wives. And possibly Marlene Dietrich but we think not.

Let us look the other way and say bon voyage.

"Bon Voyage."

What Alice Did

Now Ernest had four wives, as you know, all fine wives and they all suited Ernest very well and Ernest suited all of them very well or isn't it pretty to think so.

With Gertrude in Paris, it was different. There were not four husbands, nor any husbands at all for Gertrude. There was Alice B. Toklas. You could say Gertrude was pleased. Maybe as pleased as Ernest with four wives.

Now Alice did any number of things, a great number of things. It might have been as great a number of things as all of Ernest's wives rolled into one.

What were these things Alice did?

Oh, everything.

Alice: cooked the meals, made the beds, cleaned the house, did the shopping, drove the machine, mowed the lawn, painted the porch, repaired the roof, paved the sidewalk, plumbed the plumbing.

You name it, Alice did it.

Meanwhile, you may say, what did Gertrude do?

Gertrude geniused.

All about the house there were bells. You never saw so many bells. A real tintinnabulation.

When Alice first met Gertrude, she said she heard a bell ring inside her. It meant Gertrude was a genius.

Gertrude never let Alice forget it. Gertrude always rang a lot of bells and they were all for Alice. It almost drove Alice bats.

"Didn't you hear me ring?" Gertrude would say. "What's the matter, are you deaf?"

"You ought to be a Swiss bellringer," Alice would say.

What did Gertrude do all this time that Alice mopped the floors? Gertrude geniused. She holed up somewhere in the house and wrote her head off. That's genius for you.

Most of the writing got stacked up and nothing came of it.

Boy, you never saw such stacked-up writing.

But Alice didn't mind. "I don't mind," said Alice.

It was a pretty good arrangement. Gertrude liked it. Alice liked it. Or sort of liked it. What more could you ask?

Maybe Ernest liked his wives more but how could you tell?

The Sawmill And The Cafe

Beside Hadley, Pauline, Martha, Mary and Ernest himself, Bumby was along. He'd come over with them. They were all in Paris.

Bumby was Ernest's son. The trouble was Ernest wasn't sure who his mother was. Bumby wasn't either. Nor were the four wives.

This thing had to be worked out and the wives weren't coming up with an answer. Ernest had to come up with an answer.

"Each mother takes a day and night," Ernest said. "That day and night Bumby belongs to her. The next day and night another mother. And so on. Rotation."

"Very well," said Hadley, Pauline, Martha and Mary. "And what about you? When is your turn?"

"We won't go into that," Ernest said. "I have my prose to attend to."

Then Ernest went off to attend to his prose.

Where they all lived in Paris was over the sawmill. As sawmills go, it went. An awful lot of sawing. An awful lot of sawdust.

Sometimes Bumby cried over the sawmill and his mothers didn't hear. They weren't deaf like Gertrude said Alice was. It wasn't that, it was the sawmill. It was sawing all the time.

17

Bumby's mothers would hold him in their arms and he would squawk to beat the band. The sawmill always squawked louder than Bumby.

Meanwhile Ernest had trotted off to his prose or to the café.

Ernest would sit at the café according to the weather. The weather was always fine in Paris but sometimes finer than others. In the finer weather, he'd sit outside the café. In the weather that was only fine, he'd sit inside.

Sometimes Ernest would sit with Ford Madox Ford. But the weather had to be the very finest. It had to be outside weather.

This was so because Ernest said Ford Madox Ford didn't smell like roses. It wasn't a nice thing to say but Ernest said it. Ernest could sit with his wives or maybe Marlene and here he'd sit with Ford Madox Ford.

Ford Madox Ford changed his name on account of Ernest. His name was Ford Madox Hueffer but Ernest didn't like it.

"Ford," Ernest said, "there is another Ford in your future." After that, Ford changed his name.

Mostly Ford would gossip and tell stories and Ernest would listen and say, "Ha-ha, Ford, you ought to write that down sometime."

Then Ernest would gossip and tell stories and Ford would listen and say, "Ha-ha, Ernest, you ought to write that down sometime."

But that was only in the finest, finest weather, outside weather. Ford Madox Ford didn't smell like roses. Or so Ernest said.

Something Almost Happens

You might say it had to happen. You might say it was fate. I guess you knew as soon as you picked up this book that it would happen. Maybe even before you picked it up.

Yes, this is going to be a big chapter and we hope we are up to it. This is where Ernest and Gertrude meet.

All that has gone before is a footpath to the main road. You are about to step out on the highway, reader.

Sometimes a big truck roars along. So do be careful. We would not want to lose a reader who has been with us this long. With the most exciting part coming up. And readers are scarce these days, what with color TV and all those massage parlors.

Here was Ernest now really in Paris, in Paris in earnest, and things humming over the sawmill. He'd gotten his wives all settled in their bunks. Whether on land or sea, the wives were always in bunks.

Ernest even thought about Bumby.

"Every child should have a hobby," Ernest said. So Ernest went out and bought Bumby a hobby horse. Ernest was thrifty and spent as little as he could. Besides, he needed the money for racing.

It was always beautiful going to the races in Paris. Ernest especially liked Longchamps and went there whenever he could. He said it reminded him of a restaurant in New York.

Sometimes the wives would go to the track with Ernest. They'd each take a loaf of long French bread.

When they'd get to the track, Ernest would put one end of a loaf in the palm of his hand and rest the other against his shoulder. Then his wives lined up and did the same. Then they would all march in.

They would all laugh and it was all very gay. Ernest would laugh and his wives would laugh and the French would laugh their French laughter.

It was all beautiful to see.

But the horses seldom laughed for Ernest. Or maybe they did laugh, give Ernest a horse laugh.

"You can lead a horse to laughter," Ernest said, "but you cannot make him win."

Besides the bread, Ernest took along the wine. Ernest and his wives ate and drank and it was fine on the grass at Longchamps.

"The wine makes the horse look faster," Ernest said, "but he really isn't. It is a tragedy in our time."

So they would all go home, not with the bread and wine they came with, except it was inside them, and certainly not with the money. That is the way it is at the races.

But it was all beautiful and fun. "It was all beautiful and fun," Ernest said. Then they'd all go to the sawmill.

Ernest was settling in now. He was unpacking his prose and his hunting gear. It looked like he was in Paris to stay.

You no doubt noticed, reader, how nervous we were throughout this chapter. We honestly started out to have Ernest and Gertrude meet but it was too much for us. Nervousness. We will rest a bit, try to get over the nervousness. And then we will come back and, cross our heart, really give you the big chapter.

27 Rue de Fleurus

27 Rue de Fleurus, remember the address, reader.

Ernest didn't. But he had it written down on the little paper he held in his hot little hand.

This was the day, really and truly the day.

Ernest looked at the street numbers as he went along and looked at the paper. His wives walked behind him like Indians up in Michigan. Pauline carried Bumby.

"Voilà," shouted Ernest. He didn't know any French but he knew voilà. It meant bingo. Ernest had matched the house number with the paper number.

"Here we are, girls," Ernest said and they all stopped.

Then Ernest stepped forward and rang the bell and waited. And waited.

"She probably didn't know I was coming," said Ernest. Then he rang again and stepped back and waited again.

"Drat it," said he after a moment. Then he stepped forward and rapped on the door with his bare knuckles. That did the trick.

The door opened and a small, dark woman peered out, then drew back a bit at what she saw.

"Did you rap?" said Alice B. Toklas. "I can't hear bells too well. Too many of them."

"I am Ernest Hemingway," Ernest said.

"Hello, Ernest Hemingway," Alice said.

These are my wives, Hadley, Pauline, Martha and Mary, in order," said Ernest. "Not to mention Bumby."

"What am I supposed to do?" Alice asked.

"Aren't you Gertrude Stein?" Ernest asked.

"Land of mercy, no," answered Alice. "She's inside asleep. Was she expecting you?"

"Ahem," said Ernest. "I would expect so." Then he reached into his pocket and produced the letter from Sherwood Anderson.

"That's good enough credentials for me," Alice said.

She showed Ernest and his wives in and Bumby too. They were ushered into a very large room but Gertrude Stein was not to be seen.

What was to be seen were scads and scads of pictures all over the place. Climbing up the walls. You never saw so many pictures. All the way up to the ceiling. One of those old-timey real high ceilings too. Like in the old country.

Ernest went around looking at the pictures and so did his wives.

"Gee," said Pauline. "Like a museum."

"Shh," said Martha. "She might hear you.

You had to put your neck way back to see the highest-up ones. Meanwhile Alice went to the stairs and called up.

"Miss Stein," she called, "Mr. Hemingway is here."

"I'll be right down," Gertrude called back.

There is just too much tension building up here, reader, both for your own good and for ours also. You can feel the page crackling with it. Maybe you can stand it but we can't. We want to get a good night's sleep. Then up and at it tomorrow.

I bet you never did really expect to see Gertrude meet Ernest or did you?

The Big Scene

"I'll be right down," Gertrude called.

Yes, you have heard that before. It is pregnant with literary history, echoing down fifty years. A silver anniversary.

Then down came Gertrude Stein.

Ernest and his wives stood at attention. Bumby would have stood if he could.

Gertrude was large as Alice was small. "That is how you can tell me, I am large," Gertrude said. All bowed at her words save Alice. Alice, of course, knew she was large.

"How do you do," said Ernest.

Gertrude was dressed in her dark nightgown. She almost always dressed in her dark nightgown. Sometimes put a sweater over it.

"Be seated," said Gertrude.

They all began to look around for chairs and the truth was, there weren't enough chairs.

Pauline sat because she was holding Bumby. Gertrude sat in the biggest chair of all. There was one chair left, so Hadley sat in it and Martha and Mary sat on either arm. You might call it a Hemingway triptych. You might.

Ernest looked around and saw all the chairs occupied. Then before he knew what he was doing, he flung himself at Gertrude's feet and sat there.

"Nice pictures you have here," Ernest said, looking up at Gertrude. He pointed with his thumb back over his shoulder.

Martha giggled a little. She wasn't really the giggly Mrs. Hemingway. At one time or another, they all giggled.

"What are you painting, young man?" Gertrude asked, looking down as Ernest looked up.

There may have been just a spark then as they looked into one another's eyes. Who knows? We doubt if any Mrs. Hemingway noticed anything.

"I'm writing, mam," said Ernest, "not painting."

"Oh," said Gertrude and then paused. "Either one writes or one paints and sometimes both or neither," she said.

"That has a good ring to it," Ernest said. "Say it again."

Gertrude said it again. Then she said, "Speaking of rings, where is Alice?" Then she rang for Alice.

Alice came in from the kitchen or somewheres.

"These are the wives," Gertrude said, nodding over to the chairs where they were sitting. "Wives, this is Alice," she said.

"We already met," Mary said.

"Alice talks to the wives," Gertrude said in explanation. Then she looked directly to Alice and said, "Talk to the wives, Alice."

So it was that Alice and the wives talked, no one is sure of just what, possibly of Bumby and baking, of socks and sealing wax.

"What are you writing, young man?" Gertrude asked, looking down.

"Words," Ernest replied, looking up.

But then their voices grew softer and lower as they talked on.

Alice went and got some little cakes and wine for the wives.

"Larger portions," said Gertrude and Alice went and got larger portions for Gertrude and Ernest. They talked on, quieter and quieter.

24

After a while, Mary and Hadley shifted seats. Mary took the chair and Hadley took the arm. As they switched, Mary said, "Keep your eyes on him," and nodded in the direction of you-know-who.

"Good wine, good painting, good talk," said Ernest, his voice getting loud now. All the wives heard.

"It is about time," Martha said to the other wives. So they all stood up at once, even Pauline who almost dropped Bumby.

They all began to file out. And, a moment later, what could Ernest do but follow? He followed after, a bit shakily.

Gertrude went to the door and Alice behind her.

"Come again soon, Ernest," Gertrude said.

That was the beginning.

A Curtain Drawn

After the Hemingways were gone, Alice B. Toklas was none too pleased.

"Why do I always have to talk to the wives?" Alice asked. You could tell by the pitch of her voice she was none too pleased. In fact, she was pitching.

"You always talk to the wives, Alice. You know that," Gertrude said, trying to calm things down.

"And all those little dishes I have to wash," Alice said. "Dishes, dishes, dishes, dishes, dishes."

"Now, now," said Gertrude.

"And they left Bumby's bottle and I suppose I have to wash that too?"

"Yes," said Gertrude.

"And the big dishes, yours and Ernest's, I wash those too. Is that it?"

"Now, now," said Gertrude. "You know you always wash the dishes."

"The worst thing is, they are all my dishes," Alice said. "My very own."

"Now, Alice," said Gertrude.

26

"I'll take my dishes and go home," said Alice.

"You are home," said Gertrude. It was true. She was home.

"And I saw you making googly eyes," Alice said, almost shouting. "Googly eyes with Ernest."

"Now, Alice," said Gertrude.

"How dumb do you think those four wives are?" asked Alice.

"They know nothing," said Gertrude.

"And all that wine. All that wine. Pouring all that wine into Ernest. Now I have to wash the glasses."

"Be careful, Alice," Gertrude said.

"Now we haven't any wine left," Alice said.

"There is always more wine in the vineyard," Gertrude told her.

"But I have to pick the grapes," said Alice, "and stamp on them too."

"The grapes of France are the finest," Gertrude said.

"Why don't you sing 'La Marseillaise'?" said Alice.

We think you will agree, reader, that it is best to close down this scene right now. It looks like things are not too good and you certainly have gotten the point by this time.

We really don't care for short chapters like this one. It cuts into our daily word production. So many words a day, reader, gets the book done. And we will have to write all the harder tomorrow or the next day to make up the lost words.

But there are some chapters you just have to draw the curtain on.

BETWEEN THE ACTS

Some Literary Talk

This chapter is going to be different, reader. This we can tell you now: If you care to, you can skip this chapter.

You won't miss a thing in the story of Gertrude and Ernest. Not a thing. We give you our word on that.

We thought maybe you'd like to talk matters over with us. Not about Gertrude and Ernest but about matters in general.

We think little breaks like this are a good thing and we hope you do too. A little literary talk between the reader and author.

We admit the last few chapters have been tough on us. And probably on you, too. All that tension. Tension so thick you could cut it with a fork.

We mentioned before how nervous we have been. Building up the big scene where Ernest meets Gertrude has not been easy, we can tell you that. So much depended on it. If we could bring it off, we just might, just might, have a book.

We leave it up to you, reader. Did we or did we not pull off that scene where our two friends meet? We like to think of them as our friends.

And we like to think of you as our friend too. We do sincerely hope we brought off the large scene for you.

And if you are still with us, we want to take this opportunity to thank you for your integrity. Some readers just skip everything, don't they, reader? But not you.

And we can tell you the next chapter is going to be a dilly. Or so we hope.

ACT TWO

Scott

Ladies and gentlemen: F. Scott Fitzgerald.

You certainly all know Scott. Ernest knew Scott and Scott knew Ernest. Gertrude knew Scott too. Zelda knew Scott. You are safe in saying everyone knew Scott.

Scott is not the star of our book, as you are well aware. Ernest and Gertrude are the stars. Constellations.

But Scott is star caliber.

Sometime we would like to author a volume where Scott has the star role. But not now. Our hands are full enough taking care of Gertrude and Ernest.

But, boy, suppose we brought in Zelda too, that is in our Scott book. Wouldn't she be a hit?

But Paris is always spring and spring is always Paris. The weather good too. Real good weather. Except when it rains. But then it is good too. You can't say anything bad about Paris rain.

Ernest and Scott were sitting in a café. It was the Café des Deux Magots before they tore it down. They rebuilt it later when they heard Ernest used to go there.

"We are a couple of maggots," Scott said, joking of course.

"Speak for yourself," Ernest said. "Ha-ha."

So they sat, good friends, on the café terrace.

"Pull your foot in, Scott," Ernest said. "I don't want you tripping anybody."

It was one of Scott's lovable ways. He used to trip everybody.

Scott pulled his foot in and then ordered drinks. Then he put in a second order before the first one came. In a while the little saucers under the drinks were piled high. Scott couldn't find Ernest.

"Are you there?" Scott said.

Ernest broke down the saucers into small piles and then he could see Scott.

"There is something I have to tell you," Scott said. He had put it off as long as he could. Fortified himself. He had drunk his drinks.

"It's about Zelda," Scott said, almost in a whisper.

Ernest pulled his chair in and leaned closer, getting all the saucers out of the way.

"Zelda says my ears are too big," Scott said, his voice near to breaking.

Ernest looked at him closely, looked at his ears.

"Don't look at them now," Scott said and hid them with his hands. A tear fell among the saucers.

"They look all right to me," Ernest said. "But you can't tell. Here, let me see." He pulled Scott's hands away.

"Uh-huh," Ernest said. "But you can't be sure."

Scott put his hands over his ears again.

"Ever since my mother told me 'Little pitchers have big ears,' I have been afraid," Scott said.

"Oh, come on," Ernest said. "There's a way to find out."

"How's that?" said Scott.

"Let's go to the Louvre," Ernest said. "It's just across the river and through the trees."

"I thought it was this side of paradise," Scott said.

So Scott and Ernest went to the Louvre. Ernest had been there numerous times but Scott had never frequented it. It was all news to him.

Scott looked at the statues. He put his head to Ernest and asked quietly, "Why aren't they wearing clothes?"

"They were poor in those days," Ernest said.

Scott was looking the statues all over. "Look at the ears," Ernest said.

Scott climbed on a pedestal and looked closely at an ear. He looked down at Ernest.

"It looks pretty big to me," he said.

"Of course, Ernest said. "Of course, it's big."

Scott looked very pleased. He ran to another pedestal and started to climb it.

"Come off it," Ernest said and Scott did. But first he took a good look at the ear. "Great Gatsby!" Scott said.

"You see," Ernest said. "Your ears aren't big at all. They're closely clipped, good looking ears. Not big at all. If they were smaller, they wouldn't hold your hat up."

Scott was all smiles.

"Remember," Ernest said, "never listen to what a woman says about your ears."

Bonjour, Bonjour

"Bonjour, bonjour. I shall take a walk. Perhaps I shall talk," said Gertrude to Gertrude one day.

"Bonjour, bonjour. The weather is fine. The weather is mine," said Gertrude to Gertrude one day.

"Bonjour, bonjour. Oh, let me expound: The world, it is round," said Gertrude to Gertrude one day.

"Bonjour, bonjour. The pigeons, alas, are there on the grass," said Gertrude to Gertrude one day.

"Bonjour, bonjour. And everyone knows a rose is a rose," said Gertrude to Gertrude one day.

An Opera For Gertrude

Visitors came from everywhere. Visitors, visitors. Visitors to 27 rue de Fleurus.

Virgil Thomson came to visit Gertrude Stein. Virgil Thomson, the composer.

"I came to visit Gertrude Stein," Virgil said. Alice let him in. Gertrude gave audience to the composer.

"I would like to compose an opera," Virgil said.

"That's good," said Gertrude.

"I would like to write music for your *Four Roses in Three Acts,*" Virgil told Gertrude.

Gertrude was all flustered, all flattered. Gertrude had always liked her *Four Roses* but little did she dream anyone would make an opera of it.

No one had ever made an opera of Gertrude Stein. Not even a popular song.

"I don't know what to say," said Gertrude, taken aback.

"Just say the word," said Virgil.

"But I can't sing," Gertrude said.

"That's all right," said Virgil. "Nobody asked you."

So they had cakes and drank wine. All the visitors had cakes and wine at 27 rue de Fleurus. The rich and the poor, the big and the little, the great and the small, all came to 27 rue de Fleurus.

"Just say the word," Virgil said.

"What is the word?" asked Gertrude.

"The word is 'go'," said Virgil.

"Go," said Gertrude and Virgil got up and went.

But it was not the last Gertrude saw of Virgil Thomson. Not by any means. Virgil came often and sat with Gertrude. They talked of *Four Roses* and had little cakes and wine.

"He sure hits that bottle," Alice said after Virgil had been there several times.

"Let us hope he hits the chords as well," Gertrude said.

Then one day Virgil came and he had an announcement. *"Four Roses* is finished," Virgil said. Gertrude knew she had finished *Four Roses* long ago. Virgil meant he had finished *Four Roses* as an opera.

Gertrude Stein was very pleased. "How did you know it was finished?" she asked.

"I ran out of chords," Virgil answered. And it was true. He had run out of chords. Gertrude Stein saw the wisdom of it. Whenever she talked about the opera, she always said, "Virgil ran out of chords."

It was all fine and fun in Paris, writing opera and going skiing and having little cakes and wine. Everybody visited everybody and wrote books and painted pictures and talked and talked. The weather was always fine except when it rained and then the rain was fine, fine as needles.

"You could sew with the needles of the rain," Gertrude Stein said. It was true. And beautifully said. Gertrude Stein said it so beautifully. But Gertrude never sewed. Alice did all the sewing.

But that was not the end of *Four Roses,* that was only the beginning. *Four Roses* went to New York and it was very big. A big bouquet, you might say.

Four Roses played every night in New York and one Saturday afternoon it was on the CBS radio. The blue network, or was it red? It was sponsored by the A&P Gypsies and Milton Cross told what it was all about.

Gertrude Stein was always grateful to Milton Cross for telling what it was all about. She had often wondered.

But Gertrude Stein was even more grateful to Virgil Thomson. Whenever she spoke of him, it was with pleasure. She always told how he ran out of chords.

But you could not say Alice always spoke of Virgil with pleasure. You could not say that.

Luxembourg Gardens

One day Ernest found himself before 27 rue de Fleurus.

He rang and rapped and Alice came.

"Can Gertrude come out?" Ernest asked.

"Glad to be rid of her," Alice said. She had to be kidding, Ernest thought.

But sure enough Gertrude did appear at the door.

"Ernest," Gertrude said.

"Gertrude," Ernest said.

They had a way of saying each other's names. It was so American.

Gertrude and Ernest walked in the Luxembourg Gardens. They sat on little chairs and talked of life and literature.

"Put your foot back in," Ernest said.

Gertrude, like Scott, had a way of sitting with her foot out.

Gertrude put her foot back in.

"I wouldn't want a bicyclist running over it," Ernest said.

There was more of life and literature and Gertrude stuck her foot out again. This time a bicyclist* did run over it.

"See, what did I tell you?" Ernest said.

It looked like Gertrude had a bad foot. She tried to stand but couldn't.

"It feels all pins," Gertrude said.

"I wish I had needles to go with them," Ernest told her.

It wasn't good at all. Ernest had to get Gertrude to a doctor. He hoped he wouldn't have to carry her.

They got there somehow and the doctor looked at Gertrude's foot.

"Bicyclic conjunctivitis," the doctor said.

"I always liked conjunctions," Gertrude told him.

The doctor had to bandage Gertrude's foot four times its size. He tore off her gown at the knee. He charged plenty.

They left the doctor's and had to figure a way of getting to 27 rue de Fleurus. A cab might do it, but Ernest had no money.

"I'm poor," Ernest said. "Poor but earnest."

It didn't amuse Gertrude. It probably wouldn't have amused anyone.

Gertrude had left her purse home. And her gown was torn off at the knees.

"Now my knees are cold," said Gertrude.

"If it isn't one thing, it's another," said Ernest.

Somehow they got to 27 rue de Fleurus.

Alice came to the door and looked at Gertrude's big foot. Then she looked at Ernest.

"What have you done to Gertrude?" Alice asked.

"Nothing," said Ernest laconically.

But as he went home to the sawmill, Alice's words echoed in Ernest's ears. "What have you done to Gertrude? What have you done to Gertrude?"

What *had* he done to Gertrude?

---

*If bicyclists weren't allowed in the Luxembourg Gardens, this one was there anyhow.

Fishing In The Seine

One day Ernest decided to go fishing in the Seine. Up in Michigan, Ernest had fished and fished. But the Seine, Ernest had never fished.

Ernest had often watched the fishermen of the Seine. He had seen them gracefully cast the long poles into the river and then as gracefully pull them out.

Ernest bought the longest pole he could find in Paris and went fishing in the Seine.

The first time Ernest cast, he hit the fisherman nearest him.

"Hey, brother, watch it," the man called to Ernest.

The second time Ernest cast, he nearly caught a man on the opposite bank. Almost pulled him into the water.

"Fish your own bank," the man called to Ernest.

The third time Ernest cast, the pole was too much for him. It pulled Ernest into the Seine.

An owner of a bookstall on the bank saw Ernest fall into the water. He ran down and dived in and pulled Ernest out.

"Gee, thanks," said Ernest.

"What is your name, son?" the man asked.

"Hemingway," Ernest said.

"Hemingway," the man said, thinking a bit. "I've got your books up there," he said, nodding to the stall, "and they don't sell."

Poor Ernest. What could Ernest say? He had fallen into the river and now his books didn't sell. "Philistine," Ernest said.

The man wanted to shove Ernest in again.

"Now wait a minute," Ernest said. "Don't be hasty. Let's talk this over." They talked it over.

"I'll buy the books myself," Ernest said.

"That'll be fine by me," the man said.

He and Ernest went up the bank together. They were both all wet. Ernest bought the books.

But it had not been a good day for Ernest. He had been fishing in the Seine but had fallen in. And the man had said his books didn't sell. And he had lost his new fishing pole.

Four Marx Brothers

While Ernest was out fishing, the four Marx Brothers stopped by the sawmill. The wives were home alone. Except for Bumby, of course.

Pauline went to the door. When she saw who was there, she assumed they had come to see Ernest.

"Ernest isn't home," Pauline said.

"That's okay," Chico said. "We come to see the wives."

Well, naturally, Pauline was pleased and she bid the four Marx Brothers come in. The other wives were pleased too. Nobody came to see them, everybody came to see Ernest.

"Where's the little boy's room?" Groucho asked.

Naturally Pauline assumed Groucho wanted to brush his mustache.

"No," said Groucho, "the little boy's room."

Then Pauline got it. Groucho wanted to see Bumby's room.

Pauline showed Groucho the very small room where Bumby slept.

"That's fine," said Groucho. And Chico and Harpo and Zeppo looked too to see where Bumby slept. They all went into the little room and smiled and nodded.

The wives wondered what it was all about. What was in the little room that so pleased the Marx Brothers?

Pauline went in to see and couldn't see a thing, except that it was crowded.

Then Hadley went in and there was scarcely any room at all.

Martha had to push her way in.

Mary could just squeeze in.

It may have been Bumby's room but there wasn't any room for Bumby now.

When they were all in, Harpo went and closed the door without saying anything. He never said anything. Then he honked his horn. It was a signal.

Groucho, Chico, Harpo and Zeppo all began to chase the wives around the room.

And Hadley, Pauline, Martha and Mary let themselves be chased.

They all had a very pleasant time, those chasing and those being chased.

When it was all over, Chico played the piano. Harpo joined in on the harp.

The wives were all tickled pink. None of them could remember the last time they were chased.

But they never said a word to Ernest. They knew Ernest wouldn't like their being chased. But they liked being chased.

An American In Paris

Do you know about it, reader? Music to read by. It is a good idea. You put a record on and read. The music keeps you from falling asleep.

The record to put on while you read this book is "An American in Paris." How do you like that? Only the best. George Gershwin.

As you know, Gertrude often talked life and literature with Ernest. Sometimes music.

"Life is a cabaret," Gertrude once said.

Ernest wondered what she meant. "Yes," he said. He didn't like to show his ignorance.

But life in the sawmill, Ernest thought, certainly wasn't any cabaret.

"Yes," Gertrude said. "Life is a cabaret, old chum."

And, reader, don't forget the record, "An American in Paris." Pick it up as soon as you can.

Marlene

"Well, I'll be switched," said Ernest.

There she was. Right there in Paris. There was the Kraut.

"Kraut," Ernest said.

"Papa," said Marlene Dietrich.

They hugged and kissed on the street in Paris.

"It's too early for night-clubbing," said Ernest.

"Let's go day-caféing," said Marlene.

They went to the Dôme.

"You can go to the Dôme when you can't go home," Ernest said.

Right away Marlene got up on a table. Stood up on a table.

Ernest thought how he loved a woman who got up on a table.

Marlene stood up and sang. She sang to Ernest.

> Papa, Papa, you can papa me,
> You are all the fish in all the sea,
> Papa, Papa, all the time.

Ernest applauded. Marlene got down from the table.

Ernest thought how he loved a woman who got down from a table.

"How are your legs, keed?" Ernest asked.

"Long and lovely," Marlene said.

"Legs Diamond," Ernest said. "If your legs were diamonds, I couldn't love you more."

"You know," Marlene said, "you are my Rock of Gibraltar."

"Say it again, sweetheart," Ernest said.

They had another drink and drank a toast.

"To the Kraut and the Rock," Ernest said, raising the glass.

"To the nicest pair in Paris," Marlene said, raising the glass.

"You've got the nicest pair in Paris," Ernest said, looking under the table.

But now it was time to kiss and good-bye.

"Don't crumble on me, Rock," Marlene said, wiping her eye.

"Don't go sour on me, Kraut," Ernest said, blowing his nose.

They kissed and good-byed.

Blue Jean Tourists

"Let's play tourists, Alice," Gertrude said.

"Yes," said Alice. "Let's."

Gertrude's foot was better and she wanted to be up and about.

Life was not all dishes and dusting for Gertrude and Alice. Life could be very pleasant.

Gertrude and Alice put on blue jeans. It was part of their playing tourists.

Gertrude and Alice went down to the Seine. It was where they liked playing tourists the best.

There was a little boat went up the Seine, went down the Seine. It was the tourists' boat, no Parisians would ride it. Gertrude and Alice rode it.

The boat would go along and there was Notre Dame, there were all the bridges, there was La Tour Eiffel.

All the tourists saw and Gertrude and Alice saw.

"Oh," said Gertrude.

"Ah," said Alice.

'Oh' and 'Ah' said the tourists.

It was part of the tourists' game.

On the little boat there was a little man who sold a little hat.

The little man sold a bigger jacket too.

On the front of the little hat there was a little Eiffel tower. On the back of the bigger jacket there was a bigger Arc de Triomphe.

It was all part of the tourists' game.

Alice and Gertrude bought the little hat and the bigger jacket. Alice had this thing for hats. Gertrude had this thing for jackets.

Alice put on the hat, Gertrude put on the jacket.

"Ah," said Alice.

"Oh," said Gertrude.

It was all very pleasant being tourists. Then Gertrude and Alice went home.

They took off the little hat, took off the bigger jacket. They sat in their blue jeans.

"Oh," said Gertrude.

"Ah," said Alice.

Gertrude and Alice were remembering playing tourists.

It was all very pleasant.

At The Cinema

One day Ernest was coming home from a hard day's prose. His wives were waiting, as was their wont, at the sawmill.

Ernest decided to stop by and see Gertrude.

So it was that Ernest went to 27 rue de Fleurus and pushed the bell.

Alice came shortly, she was not very tall, and opened the door. "Did you ring?" she asked.

"Never ask for whom the bell tolls," Ernest said. He bowed slightly and asked, "Can Gertrude come out and play?"

"She's playing around inside now," Alice said. "I don't see what difference it makes."

Alice took Ernest into the big picture room and immediately left for the kitchen or somewheres.

Gertrude was seated as usual. She seldom stood. Ernest walked toward her and she lifted her hand for him. He bowed and kissed it. It was a good thing Alice was in the kitchen or somewheres.

"Tell me about your prose, Ernest," Gertrude said.

"All in good time," Ernest said. "In time. In our time."

"My time is your time," Gertrude said.

"I have come to ask you to go to the cinema," said Ernest.

"What is playing there?" inquired Gertrude.

"The Bowery Boys Meet Marshal Foch," Ernest told her.

"With Erich von Stroheim?" asked Gertrude eagerly.

"No other," said Ernest.

"I'd love to go," said Gertrude. "But first I must change my gown. And tell Alice."

Gertrude went off and Ernest looked at the pictures. Gertrude came back on and it looked like the same nightgown to Ernest. They left without saying a word to Alice.

In the cinema Ernest held Gertrude's hand the whole time. Except when he went to get popcorn.

When Ernest went to get popcorn, he got popcorn but he also got lost. He was a long time finding his way back to Gertrude.

"I got lost," Ernest said.

"You are a lost generation," Gertrude told him.

Later they walked home in the Paris moonlight. The weather was fine. They talked and talked of the film. Gertrude was of the opinion that it was fine. "Like the weather," she said.

Ernest was of the opinion that the film was fine. "Like the weather," he said.

He told Gertrude about the time Elmo Lincoln came to Michigan to make a Tarzan film.

"Yes," said Gertrude. She told Ernest of seeing Lon Chaney in *The Cabinet of Dr. Calagari.*

They were before Gertrude's doorstep now. 27 rue de Fleurus. The night was late. The moon was gone. The shadow was deep.

Whether they kissed or not, we could not say.

Gertrude let herself in with the latch key.

And, at the sawmill, when Ernest got home, there was hell to pay.

Getting Out of Corners

At the sawmill a day or two later, things were still pretty bad. One wife after another got Ernest off in a corner. It seemed to Ernest he had been in every corner of the sawmill.

"Where were you the other night, Ernest, where were you?" one wife after another asked.

But Ernest had learned from his prose. He kept his lip buttoned or almost tender buttoned. "Out," was all Ernest said.

His wives knew he had been out. His answer didn't help any. Then Ernest was sure he'd been in every corner of the sawmill. And the wives weren't letting up. Ernest had to do something.

"All right, girls," Ernest said, "let's go to the Murphys."

Ernest's wives hadn't been to the Murphys. Ernest hadn't either. But Ernest felt he knew the Murphys. Scott Fitzgerald knew the Murphys and Ernest knew Scott and everybody knew everybody in Paris and the weather was fine.

Ernest's wives knew the Murphys were pretty snazzy.

"But we haven't anything to wear," the wives said, all in one voice.

Ernest had heard that old line 1001 times before. He had read Ben Hecht's *1001 Afternoons in Chicago*.

"All you need is a bathing suit," said Ernest.

"But we don't have that either," the wives said. It was true. They didn't have a bathing suit among the four of them.

"Then go naked," Ernest said tersely.

The wives squealed with delight. "And what about you?" they said.

"I have my undershorts and my gondolier's blouse," Ernest said. Cole Porter had sent him a gondolier's blouse from Venice.

"And Zelda," said Pauline, "will Zelda be there?"

"Probably," said Ernest.

"And will she go naked too?" asked Pauline.

"Probably," said Ernest.

So that was the way it was. Ernest packed his undershorts and his gondolier's blouse and the wives packed Bumby.

"At least I am getting out of the sawmill corners," Ernest said to himself.

And they were all happy and very gay and the sun shone and the weather was fine and they were on their way to the Murphys.

Golly day, reader, can't you see what is in store for us now?

The Murphys

Now away from Paris, not too far away, was the Cap d'Antibes and here Sara and Gerald Murphy had their Villa America and a monkey named Mistigris.

Culture ran out of the ears of Sara and Gerald Murphy. Sophisticated as all hell. Money was something to laugh about and to have plenty of. Life was a song and dance.

Gerald's father had a pile. He owned the A&P. When young, Gerald worked in a New Jersey store for experience.

In New Jersey, Gerald wore a white jacket and apron. With pants underneath, of course. He couldn't keep anything in his pockets. He feared the manager would think he was pilfering. Later he married and went to Paris.

But Gerald never kept anything in his pockets. He carried a bright colored square of silk and kept his personal belongings in it. Sometimes he would forget and use the square for a handkerchief. Then his personal belongings would fall all over the place.

Sara always wore a long strand of pearls, even while bathing. Whether in the tub or in the ocean.

Sara had a fetching way of tossing the pearls backward over her shoulders. Once she lassoed Gerald and he had to Charleston twenty minutes to break loose.

The Murphys loved folk songs and jazz. Sara would let down her shoulder straps and sing "Hallelujah, I'm a Bum."

Gerald had a schooner built a hundred feet long, not to drink from but to sail in.

All was grace and graceful living at Antibes, at Villa America. The sun caressed the golden sand and the waves whispered to the shore. The weather was fine. There was never anything but fine weather.

To this earthly paradise came the Hemingways.

Those Who Came

The A&P Gypsies played on and on and to the Villa America that year these people came:

From Good Egg came Picasso with his mistress, Fernande, and everyone said how handsome he was.

Picasso looked dark and strong, in fact, he was dark and strong. Some said he should bathe more. His hair fell over one eye like Veronica Lake, only she was light where he was dark.

Picasso wanted to paint everything but Gerald said no. Gerald said everything had been freshly painted and didn't need a second coat.

Still Picasso persisted. He painted the beach umbrellas to look like toadstools. Gerald put the umbrellas down and told him to watch it. Picasso told him what he could do with his beach umbrellas.

And from Bad Egg with his high-button shoes and hair parted in the middle came H. L. Mencken. Some called him Henry and others called him a lot of things. He put all the things in a book.

Everywhere Henry went he carried a green magazine. Like Gerald's square. But Gerald's square wasn't always green.

The magazine was *The American Mercury* and cost fifty cents which was a lot. Still Henry didn't pay his contributors much.

Everyone said Henry looked like he'd just gotten off the boat. It was true. Henry did look like he'd just gotten off the boat. Even when he got back on the boat.

And Jack Dempsey and Gene Tunney came too. They got in first one fight and then another. Billy Sunday came and stayed to Monday. Ethel Barrymore came and brought her brothers.

Henry Ford came and drove a Chevrolet. Rockefeller came, the old thin one, and gave everyone a dime.

Caresse Crosby came and everyone caressed her.

Gene Stratton Porter and Knut Hamsun came together. The Bobbsey Twins came. John Philip Sousa came and brought his band.

Galli-Curci came and sang. Madame Schumann-Heink came and danced. Henny Youngman came and played the violin.

Dizzy and Dazzy Vance came, Mahatma and Indira Gandhi came. Laurel and Hardy came. Al and Kate Smith came.

Matisse, Juan Gris and Andrew Wyeth all came together. Clayton, Jackson and Durante came.

Tom Edison came with his electric light. Tom Swift came with his electric car.

Dante came with a comedy.

Shoeless Joe Jackson and Sliding Billy Watson came.

Franklin D. Roosevelt, assistant secretary of the Navy, came with his wife and children.

Dorothy Thompson came with her husband. Upton Sinclair came with Lanny Budd.

Edgar Poe came with his raven and Annabel Lee.

William Faulkner came with a rose for Emily, but Miss Dickinson wasn't there.

John L. Lewis came with his eyebrows.

Bobby Jones came with his knickers, Bill Tilden came with his flannels.

Borrah Minevitch came with his Rascals.

John Barth came with Anne Tyler.

Michael Arlen came with his green hat.

Tom Wolfe came with Thomas Wolfe.

e e cummings came with his lower case. Henry James came with his upper class.

Mardi O'Shaughnessy, Jonathan Baumbach, Alan Hines, Charles Johnson and Raymond Federman came with the Fiction Collective.

Barney Google came with his goo-goo-googly eyes.

Corrigan came the wrong way.

Elinor Glyn came in sin. Came Ogden Nash and was a smash. Came Vernon Duke and played a uke. Played "April in Paris."

George Arliss came as Disraeli. Al Jolson came as Joe Louis. Primo Carnera came as Tom Thumb.

Svengali came with Trilby. Rasputin came with Mad Man Muntz.

King Kong came with Fay Wray. Tom Mix came with Tony. Rin-Tin-Tin came by himself.

All these people came to Villa America that year, the short and the fat, the tall and the thin, the light and the dark, the bald and the toupéed, the young and the old, the living and the dead.

Jaws

To this earthly paradise came the Hemingways.

Sara knew it was Ernest by his fine, hard prose. Ernest knew it was Sara by her pearls. He bowed and kissed her hand. He had been doing a lot of hand-kissing lately.

Then Gerald strolled by, carrying his silk square. He and Ernest shook hands.

"Living good is the best kind of living," Ernest said.

"You can say that again," said Gerald.

Then Ernest introduced his wives in order. Bumby was playing in the sand. Ernest introduced him and Bumby rose.

"The son also rises," said Ernest.

Then servants appeared from everywhere and little cakes and wine were all over the place. Little cakes and wine were big in Paris that year. Big in Antibes, too.

Then the door at Villa America opened and out on the bright sand came Monty Woolley.

All the Hemingway wives squealed at once. They had all seen Monty in the movies. They liked him particularly as Charlie Chan.

Monty shook hands with everyone. The wives were thrilled. Monty had just washed his beard.

Then it was swimming time and Mistigris, the Murphys' pet monkey, spoke. "It's time for swimming," he said. Gerald had taught him how to speak. It was most charming.

"Last one in is a monkey," Mistigris said.

All at once the wives pulled their dresses over their heads. They were all all bare and ready to swim. They clasped hands and ran into the water.

Monty Woolley had some kind of an attack. Gerald made him sit down and take it easy.

Sara, Gerald and Ernest went into the house to change. Monty was still sitting down, taking it easy.

Then Sara and Gerald came out on the sand, attired beautifully for bathing. Sara wore her pearls and Gerald carried his silk square and a cane. They walked into the surf together.

Ernest came out a bit later, looking fine in his gondolier's blouse and undershorts. He went down the beach and up to his knees into the water.

The wives all stopped for a moment and turned to Ernest. They splashed him and called out, "Ernest is a monkey, Ernest is a monkey." Ernest was a monkey, he was the last one in.

Monty Woolley watched it all carefully, especially if one of the wives came too much out of the water.

They all romped and played and it was lovely under the sun and in the water. The water was fine. No one would have guessed that there had been a false spring.

Then Mistigris on the beach sighted something out in the water. He was greatly excited.

"Shark," he cried. He was always reading books.

All the wives heard. They turned tail at once and beat it back to the beach. Both Sara and Gerald strolled in, hurrying just a little. Only Ernest stayed in the water, looking out to sea. Then he too turned and came in.

Ernest went up to Gerald. "Where is your boat, Gerald?" Ernest said.

"It is over yonder," Gerald said, pointing to the schooner. Then he remembered himself. It wasn't polite to point. He dropped his hand quickly.

"Too big," Ernest said. Then he saw the Murphys' canoe nearby, with the harpoon in it.

Ernest rushed toward the canoe, got in and pushed off, harpoon and all.

They all stood on the beach watching.

"Look at that old man and the sea," said Martha. The other wives could only shake their heads.

Women On Pedestals

You could say there were tense moments on the shore. You could say that.

All the wives and the two Murphys stared out to sea. Mistigris did too. Gerald made Monty stay a distance away. After all, the wives were out of the water and out of their clothes.

But the canoe and Ernest were not to be seen. He had gone out and out. The last they had seen of him and the canoe, he had the harpoon poised high over his head. Then he and the canoe disappeared. On the shore all stood and stared out to sea.

Then it was Mistigris. He started to jump and clap his hands and point.

"Don't point," Gerald said.

But Mistigris paid no attention. He jumped and clapped and pointed. "Ernest, Ernest," he said.

They all looked and sure enough it was Ernest. The canoe had been turned about and Ernest was paddling back in.

"It's our Ernest," said Mary. The other wives echoed her.

As he came nearer, Ernest waved. Then he jumped out the canoe, pushed it to shore. He reached into the canoe and picked up something. Then, carrying the object, he came towards them.

"A shark's fin," said Ernest, carrying the trophy high.

They all looked at the shark's fin.

"It's plastic," Gerald said. They all looked and saw it was plastic.

"Kid stuff," said Gerald. "The kids are doing it all the time. Scaring everybody.

Ernest was as mad as hops. He looked at Gerald, his face hard and taut as his prose.

"Oh, come off it, Ernest," Gerald said.

And, don't you know, Ernest did come off it. He wasn't mad anymore. He knew you couldn't fool anybody with a plastic fin. Not when it was out of the water.

But the weather was fine, the sun going down now though the sand still shone and they laughed and swam and sang songs on the beach. Then the wives became cold.

"Wait a minute," said Gerald, seeing their gooseflesh. Then he led them all off the beach and into the garden up by the house. Sara and Ernest came too.

"I have just the place to dry you and warm you," Gerald said to the wives. He thought of everything.

In each of the four corners of the garden, there stood a statue on a pedestal. Each statue was of a woman. One was spring, another summer, the third autumn and winter was the last. The figures shone in the sun.

Gerald went about the garden and lifted each statue from its pedestal.

"For you," Gerald said, bowing to the wives.

Then he went and placed his hands on Pauline's waist and lifted her high. There she stood where the statue had been.

"I always wanted to be put on a pedestal," Pauline said.

Then he lifted the others just as he had Pauline. Each stood on a pedestal in a corner of the garden. They glistened and warmed in the sun.

Gerald went to the center of the garden to make an announcement. He stood with his arms raised and slowly turned full circle.

"You are all spring," he said. "May there never be autumn or winter."

"Wait a minute," said Ernest.

Gerald looked toward Ernest and Ernest looked toward Gerald.

Then slowly Ernest spoke. "Let me do that," he said.

Gerald bowed and stepped aside and gave Ernest the center of the garden.

Ernest raised his arms and slowly turned full circle.

"You are all spring," he said. "May there never be autumn or winter."

Each of the wives gave a little squeal.

Then a door of the Villa America burst open and into the garden ran Zelda Fitzgerald.

Zelda

Zelda ran over to Ernest and gave him a kiss. Then she jumped on the little table that stood in the center of the garden.

"Music, maestro, please," Zelda called out.

Over to the side, the A & P Gypsies began to play. Gerald always kept them on hand.

Zelda started to Charleston with Ernest there at her feet. The orchestra blared away.

Shining in the sun, the wives on their pedestals all joined in and danced the Charleston. It was charming to see.

Then Zelda reached up and pulled off her dress and then her whatnots. She kicked in the direction of Ernest and almost kicked his nose. Then she threw her dress and whatnots over Ernest's head.

From out the Villa America and into the garden came Scott Fitzgerald. He had on the gondolier's blouse Cole Porter had sent from Venice. He looked and saw Zelda dancing without her clothes. He looked and saw Ernest standing with Zelda's clothes over his head.

Scott went to have a word with Ernest. He got there just as Ernest's head came out of Zelda's clothes. Scott decided not to have a word with Ernest. Instead he swung hard and caught Ernest one on the nose. Ernest went down.

All the wives squealed and jumped off their pedestals. They started chasing Scott around the garden. They ran pretty fast and almost caught Scott. After all, they were unadorned and unencumbered.

Gerald called each wife by name and asked her to stop chasing Scott.

The music kept on playing, the wives kept on chasing Scott and Zelda kept on dancing.

"I think I'd better get Monty," Gerald said to Sara.

Gerald went to the beach where he'd made Monty stay. He brought him back to the garden.

Gerald and Monty caught two wives apiece and made them put their clothes on. Monty liked catching them but didn't like it when they put clothes on.

But it gave Scott a chance to catch his breath.

Gerald and Monty took the wives into the house and then came back to survey the situation.

Scott had caught his breath. He went over to look closer at Zelda's dancing. Zelda kicked out at Scott and almost kicked his nose.

Zelda always kicked at noses. It was one of her charming ways.

Scott caught Zelda's ankle and pulled her off the table. Scott fell down and Zelda fell on top of him.

Mistigris ran over and pulled Zelda off Scott. Monty wished he could have done it.

Scott got up and brushed off his gondolier's blouse. It was just like the one Ernest wore.

Gerald came over and asked Zelda to put on her clothes. Monty had asked him not to ask her.

Scott kept brushing his blouse and Zelda put on what clothes she could find. Her bra was missing.

69

Then Gerald and Monty went over to Ernest. They picked him up head and feet and carried him into the house.

Both Scott's and Ernest's gondolier blouses were the worse for wear. Scott thought he might call up Cole Porter and get new ones.

So the sun went down on Villa America and Sara and Gerald Murphy and their guests were all indoors. The weather had been fine.

But the day wasn't over yet. Not by a long shot.

The Green Light

They had scarcely gotten indoors when the party began.

There were always parties at the Murphys. No one knew just how the parties came about. It all seemed to have something to do with a gracious way of living. Sara would wave a wand or Gerald would clap his hands and a score of servants would appear.

It was champagne all over the place. Then three A & P Gypsies stood up and sounded their trumpets. A fanfare.

The headwaiter came in with a tray of caviar molded into a figure. It was Babe Ruth at the bat. There was something so American about the Murphys.

Everyone was there and fully clothed. Monty tried to get Zelda to lean over. He knew she'd lost her bra. All the Hemingway wives were there. Their gooseflesh was gone.

Even Ernest had somehow miraculously revived. He'd washed out his gondolier's blouse and put it on again. His nose was all tied up.

Scott was in full dress with ruffles. Zelda kept tripping over her skirt.

The Countess de Chemise had come and Monty Woolley asked her to dance. Everyone said they were a lovely couple, he with his long white beard, she nearly bald.

Archibald MacLeish dropped in with John Dos Passos but they began to fight. Each invited the other outside and they were gone before anyone knew they were there.

It was a fine evening. The guests floated in and out of the house, danced in the ballroom, danced on the terrace. Sara flipped her necklace, Gerald folded his square.

Scott spotted Ernest across the room. He went over to him and tried to autograph his nose.

Ernest was quite sensitive about such things. He tried to kick and punch Scott both at the same time. It was a difficult maneuver and Ernest fell to the floor.

Ernest's wives hurried over to help him up. They explained that Scott was just an overgrown boy. Ernest said the floor was too slippery. He said his nose hurt too much to fight.

The Countess de Chemise and Monty swept by and everyone applauded their dancing. Scott dropped two raw oysters into the front of the Countess's dress. She stopped dancing and stood perfectly still. Then she grabbed Monty's beard and shrieked to high heaven.

Then Scott strolled to the fireplace. He picked up one of Sara's fine crystal glasses and threw it into the fire. He said he liked to hear the sound as it crashed. It was one of Scott's lovable ways.

Then he started throwing other glasses in, one after the other. When three dozen lay in the fireplace, Gerald strolled over.

"We don't do that, Scott," he said. Then he told Scott he couldn't use their bathroom for three weeks. It was the gracious way Gerald did things.

Then Zelda pushed Scott in the swimming pool. He climbed out and pushed Zelda in. It was the charming way they had with one another.

Sara and Gerald counted the people still on their feet. There weren't many. The caviar Babe Ruth had just about struck out. Nearly all the champagne had been drunk or spilled. The party was ending.

The Hemingway wives didn't want to go home with Ernest. They said his nose looked funny. Somehow Ernest rounded them up.

The Fitzgeralds were still rather wet. Scott said his ruffles would never dry. Gerald said he didn't know it had been raining. He always said just the right thing. Scott held a parasol over Zelda as they left.

Archibald MacLeish and John Dos Passos had come and gone and no one was the wiser.

Sara and Gerald counted and only the Countess de Chemise and Monty were missing. Gerald found them in the billiard room. Monty was trying to get the oysters from the Countess's gown.

Sara and Gerald strolled down to the beach. They looked out at the green light at the end of the pier. They wondered when it would turn red.

We are all ships driven endlessly back and forth across great seas.

BETWEEN THE ACTS

A Thank You Pause

Reader, could you go for a pause in our story about this time? We sure could. There is something about these big parties that gets us down.

We must be at about the half-way mark at this time. In our writing, that is. That is, if we can go on. We certainly hope so.

We want to tell you, reader, how much of a help you are to us. We just couldn't go on without you. Quite often we visualize you reading this. It spurs us on.

Ernest said he once wrote a book in ten days. We will tell you this, reader: we have been out on the track (notice how we occasionally use sports metaphors) for more than ten days already. And our book at this point is only half finished.

I guess we will have to settle for things the way they are. Which means, reader, that we are not Ernest. We are sure you will agree.

Just leaning back and chatting with you is a help. It helps us build up our strength, we hope. Some writers think when they half finish a book, they've got it made.

We want to tell you, reader, we don't think we've got it made. We don't even know if we've got it half made.

At this point, we know we have got to fight harder than ever.

Just so as to not let you down, reader.

And if, about this time, you have begun to wonder about Gertrude, we will say she is all right, thank you. And we will get back to her as soon as we possibly can. You know we wouldn't forget her. And we do thank you, reader, for your interest and patience.

ACT THREE

Pining For Ernest

We said we would tell you about Gertrude and we will right off. We said that everything was all right. That may have been a slight exaggeration. Alice was still going on about the dishes. And she wasn't too happy about Basket either.

Basket was Gertrude's pet poodle. Alice took the most care of him and Gertrude took the least.

When Gertrude first got the dog, she said he looked like a basket. Alice said he didn't look like a basket at all. Every day they'd argue about it.

If they didn't argue about Basket's name, they'd argue about taking him for a walk. Alice took him for a walk sixteen days straight.

"There is no reason why I should take him for a walk the seventeenth day," Gertrude said.

Then if they didn't argue over Basket's name or taking him for a walk, they'd argue over the dishes. Once Alice broke a dish and Gertrude said she hoped she'd break them all.

"I'm not Scott Fitzgerald," Alice said. It was true. She wasn't Scott Fitzgerald.

That was the way it was at 27 rue de Fleurus. It wasn't really the dog or the dishes that was wrong with Gertrude. What it was, she was pining for Ernest.

Now a young reader may think that pining is not the right word to use here. A young reader may think that people do not pine anymore. What with blue jeans and the pill, he may well be right. Maybe people do not pine anymore.

But you have to remember that this was in Paris years ago and Gertrude certainly pined. She pined for Ernest.

That was the scene at 27 rue de Fleurus.

Sawdust At The Sawmill

At the sawmill everything wasn't exactly hunky-dory either. Ernest's nose was tied up and he didn't particularly care to go out in public.

The wives were bickering all over the place. They still wanted to know where Ernest went that night he got home late. They wanted to know, too, about Zelda. What did she mean by throwing her dress and whatnots over Ernest's head?

Ernest had learned from his prose. He said nothing.

Then the wives bickered about Bumby. They wanted Ernest to take him out for a walk.

Ernest said he wouldn't take Bumby out with his nose.

The wives said there was nothing wrong with Bumby's nose.

"Not Bumby's nose, my nose," said Ernest.

Then the wives started on something else. They started bickering over F. Puss.

F. Puss was the Hemingway cat.

"What does the F. stand for?" Hadley asked.

"It's her first name," said Ernest.

"F. isn't a name, it's an initial," said Hadley. "What does the initial stand for?"

"I don't remember," Ernest said.

Hadley told him he'd have to take care of the cat himself. The wives had enough with Bumby. And they always had to keep dusting everything. This was because of the sawmill.

Ernest told them if they wanted to take care of him, they'd have to take care of the cat too.

Pauline and Martha and Mary all chimed in. They said Ernest and the cat could take care of themselves. And they said they were tired of dusting.

Ernest had had enough. He took Bumby and F. Puss and went out walking with his nose tied up. What did his wives want him to do? Dust.

The Mystery Of It All

Though trouble persisted at 27 rue de Fleurus and at the sawmill, life continued its gracious way at Villa America. Neither Scott nor Ernest had come back. Scott had lost bathroom privileges and Ernest had the nose problem.

But there were always other guests at Villa America. Isadora Duncan came with her brother Raymond. Raymond was always losing his sandals strolling about the Villa. Once he lost his toga.

Isadora tried to draw Gerald to her. She put her veil about his neck but Gerald didn't go for it. He merely folded his square. Besides, Sara was watching.

And Rudolph Valentino came too. He played scenes from *The Shiek.* And Rudy Vallee came at the same time and sang. A sort of double feature. Sara loved the "Maine Stein Song." She said she always wanted to go to college at Heidelberg.

Hasn't it been good, reader, to catch up on all our friends, on what is going on at 27 rue de Fleurus, at the sawmill and at the Villa? We think all writers should try to catch their readers up on things, don't you?

Now, reader, you know as much about what is going on as we do. Maybe more. We wish we knew more. We wish we knew what direction life was carrying all our friends. But that is the great part of it all, the mystery of it all. You never know what is going to happen next. We certainly don't.

Words of Love

Yes, things were getting a bit rough on Ernest. He just had to get out of the house. He wanted to see Gertrude but he was sensitive of his appearance. He was afraid Gertrude couldn't stand a bandaged-up man.

What Ernest did was write Gertrude a note. It said:

Dear Gertrude,
I love you.
Sincerely,
Ernest

It was so like Ernest. Every word so direct, so terse. Ernest was a terse man.

Then he took the Katzenjammer Kids from the Sunday papers. Ernest loved the Katzenjammer Kids and he knew Gertrude loved them too. He took the note and the Katzenjammer Kids and put them in an envelope.

Ernest walked to 27 rue de Fleurus. He slipped the envelope under the door. Ernest didn't want Gertrude to see his nose. He didn't want Alice to see it either.

Later the same day Alice found the envelope and took it to Gertrude. Gertrude opened it carefully. She didn't want Alice to see anything. But Alice couldn't help seeing the Katzenjammer Kids.

"What's this Katzenjammer Kids business?" Alice asked.

Gertrude smiled a little slyly. "They remind me of home," Gertrude said.

"But you are home," said Alice.

"That's what I mean," Gertrude told her.

But Gertrude was careful about the note. She put it on a high shelf where Alice never dusted. It was safe there.

Then Gertrude wrote a note. She said:

> *Dear Ernest,*
> *When can I see you?*
> *Yours,*
> *Gertrude*

Gertrude really wanted to write more. But she worried that Ernest wouldn't like it. So she followed his style, a style as direct as his kiss on her hand, as direct as his eyes on hers.

Gertrude thought of carrying the note to the sawmill. Then she thought: "Why should I do it? I'll get Alice." She rang a bell and Alice came.

"Please take this to Ernest, Alice," she said. "At the sawmill. Wait for an answer. Try not to let the wives see you."

Alice didn't mind too much. It gave her a chance to get away from the dishes.

On the way Alice thought to herself: "Gertrude is a little off her rocker. How can I wait for an answer and not let the wives see me?" Alice had something there. Maybe Gertrude was a little off her rocker. But that is what love does.

Alice rang the sawmill bell and just by chance Ernest came.

Alice gave him the note and waited for him to read it.

On the same sheet of paper, Ernest wrote back:

> *Dear Gertrude,*
>> *Not today. I have a bad cold.*
>>> *Sincerely,*
>>> *Ernest*

He folded it up and put it in the same envelope and gave it to Alice.

"What's the matter with your nose?" Alice asked.

"I have a bad cold," Ernest said. "But don't mention my nose to Gertrude."

Then he went inside and shut the door.

"He could have said good-bye," Alice said.

Inside, Ernest really caught it.

"What's that Toklas woman doing here?" Martha said.

"She's supposed to talk to the wives," said Pauline.

"Why didn't she come in?" said Mary.

"What's she doing hanging around the sawmill?" Hadley said.

Ernest said: "She brought Bumby's bottle back." It wasn't true but it was pretty quick thinking. With four wives you had to do pretty quick thinking.

Sylvia and Joyce

Yes, Ernest was very restless at the sawmill. He just had to get out of the house.

"I haven't anything to read," Ernest said. It was true. He didn't have anything to read. He had his own stories but he knew the plots.

"I'm going to see Sylvia," Ernest said.

"Who is Sylvia?" Pauline asked.

Ernest got down Shakespeare and read "Who is Sylvia" to Pauline. Then he said, "Does that answer your question?" He went out and slammed the door lightly. With four wives it was better not to slam the door hard.

Ernest was on his way to see Sylvia Beach.

Sylvia was a little girl with a big bookstore. It was called Shakespeare and Company.

Sylvia was a girl who was born in Baltimore but left as soon as she could. Even before she could walk. Then she came to Paris and opened this bookstore.

The big thing about Sylvia was she was buddy-buddy with James Joyce. She was the little girl who published Joyce's big book, *Ulysses.* She sold a lot of copies over the counter. Under too.

Sylvia had done Joyce a favor by publishing the book but Joyce didn't think so. He thought he had done her a favor. That's the way things are sometimes.

The thing of it was with James Joyce he had just about the biggest name there was. Only if Shakespeare had been living, he would have had a bigger name.

The thing of it was, too, everybody wanted to meet James Joyce. The big trouble was James Joyce didn't want to meet anybody. Except Samuel Beckett, who wore the same size shoes as Joyce.

Ernest certainly wanted to meet James Joyce. He had wanted to meet James Joyce since he was a little boy. Since Ernest was a little boy, not James Joyce.

That was one of the reasons Ernest was on his way to Sylvia's. The other was he didn't have anything to read.

"Hi, Sylvia," said Ernest as he walked into the store.

"Hi, Ernest," Sylvia said.

"Is James Joyce coming in today?" Ernest asked. He had asked Sylvia many times before but he had had no luck.

"Sure enough," Sylvia said. "It just so happens James Joyce is coming in today."

Ernest smiled all over. He had very good teeth.

"The trouble is," Sylvia said, "he doesn't want to meet anybody."

"Shucks," said Ernest.

"But I'll tell you what," said Sylvia. "I just might arrange it." She pointed to the back of the store.

"You sort of hide back there," she said. "Crouch down under the skylight."

"Sure enough," said Ernest. He went back and crouched down in the corner under the skylight. It wasn't very comfortable. He couldn't read and he didn't have a pencil to write with. He kept watching the front of the store.

In a while the door opened and in walked James Joyce. Sylvia

91

went to greet him but on her way she heard this crash. She looked around and saw Ernest with his head through the skylight.

Sylvia was torn for a moment between James Joyce and Ernest. She decided Ernest needed her more. She went to him and there was glass all over the place. Ernest's head was bloody and not unbowed. He'd gotten all excited when he saw James Joyce.

James Joyce found his way to the back of the store and asked Sylvia what was going on. He couldn't see very well at all. Ernest stood with his head in the skylight or where the skylight had been.

Sylvia didn't explain to James Joyce what was going on. She just went ahead and telephoned. She thought it best. Ernest was really all cut up.

When the ambulance came, both Sylvia and James Joyce helped Ernest to get into it. James Joyce couldn't see very well. He thought Ernest was a woman about to have a baby.

Sylvia and James Joyce rode in the ambulance with Ernest.

At the hospital the doctors went over Ernest's head with a fine-tooth comb. They got most of the glass out. Then they tied up Ernest's head with bandages a mile long.

It was in the hospital room that Ernest finally met James Joyce.

James Joyce asked, "How are the matter and boyby coming along?"

Sylvia said it hadn't been such a bad day after all. At least Ernest had met James Joyce.

'Yes," said Ernest, "but I didn't get anything to read."

One Of The Nicer Things

How do you like it so far, reader?

Why don't you lie down and take a nap. Or go to bed early tonight?

It might do you good. If we take a nap, it helps us. Only we don't want to ever get up again.

Books are very nice things. A book is one of the nicer things we know. And the nicest thing about a book is how it waits for you.

Just think of all those books that wait for you. Whether you've read them or not. *War and Peace, Huckleberry Finn, Remembrance of Things Past, The Wind in the Willows.*

If you wish it to, a book will wait for you forever. Find a girl who'll do that.

Why don't you take a nap and when you wake up you can continue this exciting book.

But don't sleep too long.

Going Off Somewheres

Now with his head and nose bandages, it was all the more difficult for Ernest to see Gertrude. Alice kept running notes back and forth like hotcakes.

First Ernest said his cold had gotten worse. Then he wrote that he had pneumonia. But Gertrude was persistent. Gertrude wanted to see him whether or no.

Ernest thought he might say he was going to jail. He decided against it. After all, he did want to see Gertrude sometime. When the bandages were off.

At last Gertrude grew desperate. She wrote: "Come under any circumstance. Come under any circumstance."

Ernest wrote back: "I will, I will."

Ernest got out of the house somehow that night. He went over to 27 rue de Fleurus. Alice was hopping mad but she let him in.

Gertrude and Ernest ran into one another's arms. It was beyond the hand-kissing stage. Alice was off in the kitchen or somewheres.

"I like your bandages, Ernest," Gertrude said. Ernest wondered why he had been so foolish about bandages. Gertrude liked them.

Gertrude and Ernest talked and talked.

"We have to go off somewheres together," Gertrude said.

Ernest said, "I wouldn't mind going off somewheres together."

"Where could we go off?" Gertrude asked.

"We could go off to Spain," Ernest said. "The bulls are about to run at Pamplona."

"Ah, Spain," Gertrude said. "Beer and wienerschnitzel." It was her little joke. It was very little.

So they talked late and late into the night and laid their plans carefully. After all, there was Alice. And the four wives.

Here Comes The Bull

The tryst was set for eight o'clock the following evening. Ernest tiptoed carefully out of the house. He carried F. Puss with him. F. Puss was enclosed in a very nice cat-carrier. Ernest had bought the cat-carrier that very day. He had kept it hidden in the sawmill. That wasn't easy with four wives.

Ernest took his flashlight and checked the tires on the Stutz Bearcat. Ernest always drove an open-top Stutz Bearcat. It had a bumper sticker that said:

DON'T GET STUCK WITH HOOVER

It was best to check the tires, Ernest knew. They went flat quite frequently. Ernest put the cat-carrier with F. Puss in it into the back seat.

Ernest tooled over to 27 rue de Fleurus. There was a light in an upstairs window. Gertrude had said there would be a light in an upstairs window. A ladder was placed beside the window, leaning against the house. Gertrude had Alice put it there at dusk.

Ernest had scarcely stopped the Stutz when Gertrude appeared at the window. She waved to Ernest who flashed the flashlight up upon her. Then she opened the window and got out on the ladder.

Gertrude had a dog-carrier with her. Basket was in it. She had to come down the ladder with one hand because she was carrying Basket.

Ernest got out of the machine and stood at the foot of the ladder, steadying it for Gertrude.

Then Gertrude had to go up again to get her suitcase.

Ernest thought about Gertrude. She was truly a romantic. After all, she could have come out the front door.

Gertrude came down again with the suitcase. She and Ernest kissed hurriedly. Ernest put Basket on the back seat with F. Puss, both in their carriers. He put the suitcase in too. He opened the door on one side for Gertrude, then he got in the other side.

They were ready to start for Spain. For Pamplona. Ernest put on his goggles. They were hard to get on over his bandages. Gertrude pulled her linen duster about her.

"Ole," said Ernest.

Gertrude said, "Ole."

It was all the Spanish they knew and they weren't too sure of that.

It was quite a pleasant trip, albeit a bit dusty. Ernest had only to change tires fourteen times. What's more he forgot the jack that held up the machine. But it was no great matter.

Gertrude would get out and lift one corner of the Stutz off the ground. Then Ernest could readily change the tire.

Ernest was right. They arrived in Pamplona the very day of the running of the bulls.

"Do you want to run with the bulls?" Ernest asked.

"You can run," Gertrude said, "but I think I'd rather not."

"Okay," said Ernest.

"Just get us a nice hotel," Gertrude said. "A room with a balcony. Then I can sit out and watch."

Ernest did just as Gertrude bid. It was a nice room with a nice balcony. Gertrude sat out on it and Ernest went down the street to find the bulls.

97

Then Gertrude heard a great hollering.

"Here comes the bull, here comes the bull," they hollered. In Spanish, of course.

Gertrude looked down and saw Ernest running to break his neck. The bull ran right behind him. Ernest ran with a rose between his teeth. Just as he passed Gertrude he tossed the rose up to her but kept running fast. He knew Gertrude liked roses.

Gertrude saw Ernest disappear around the corner with the bull close behind him. She got up and went in the hotel room. She put the rose in a glass with water in it.

When Ernest came back to the hotel that night, the seat of his pants was all snagged. Gertrude said she'd mend it for him but she forgot the needle.

Ernest kissed Gertrude passionately.

Then he went out on the balcony to sleep. He told Gertrude he wanted to see if the bulls ran at night.

A Swift Kick

At dawn Gertrude got up and went out on the balcony.

Ernest was curled up in a ball against the night air. Gertrude saw a bit of frost on his ear.

She went inside to get a blanket. She spread it tenderly over him. She went back in and changed the water in the glass that held the rose. Then she crept back into bed for a little extra shut-eye.

Before she'd gotten to sleep, Gertrude heard a rumpus on the balcony. It was Ernest trying to get up. The night air had gotten to him.

Gertrude got out of bed and went over and took his hand. With one pull she got Ernest to his feet. But he couldn't straighten up. He was bent double.

Ernest put his hand on his hip and walked about the room bent double.

"The old rheumatiz," Ernest said.

It was a disturbing sight. Ernest walked a bit, his back toward Gertrude. His back was really toward the ceiling.

Gertrude went over and gave him a swift kick.

It did the trick. It was just what Ernest needed. He straightened up immediately.

Then Ernest would have gotten dressed but he already was.

This was the big day, the day of the big bullfight. Of course, Gertrude and Ernest were going.

"I've got to see a man down the street," Ernest said and went out.

Ernest saw a man down the street that did decorating. He told the man what he wanted.

The man decorated Ernest's head bandage with bull's horns. Painted them right on the bandage, very realistic.

Then the man painted Ernest's nose bandage like a tomato. The man said it was an old Spanish bullfight custom.

It was all in fun, of course. Ernest wanted to surprise Gertrude.

When Ernest got back to the hotel, Gertrude was dressed in her best. She wore her pants suit with the embroidered necktie.

When Ernest came into the room with his bull's horns and tomato, Gertrude was really surprised.

"Is it really you, Ernest?" she said.

"It is I," said Ernest. He gave an imitation Spanish dance but it wasn't a very good imitation.

They had breakfast at the hotel, apple pie with cheese. It was an old Spanish bullfight day custom, the waitress said. Gertrude thought they were getting rid of last night's dessert.

Gertrude and Ernest hopped a trolley to the arena. It was a colorful ride. Everyone was going to the bullfight. They saw many who had their noses decorated like tomatoes.

"But none is so large as yours," Gertrude told Ernest. He laughed.

They entered the arena then. It was such a big day. Gertrude could not believe it all. She looked at Ernest beside her. Then she believed it all.

Going for Coca-Cola

Ernest had the best seats, right down front. Paid plenty for them.

"Living good is a good revenge," Ernest said.

"It is, it is, it is," Gertrude told him.

There was a lot going on. Picadors, matadors, troubadours going up and down the aisles selling pizzas. People everywhere. Gertrude looked around. At the people in the stands, that is.

Gertrude saw Mabel Dodge Luhan and Joyce Carol Oates. Gertrude waved to them and they waved back. They had come from California to see the bullfight.

D.H. Lawrence and T.S. Eliot were with the women. Gertrude saw them and told Ernest.

Ernest waved. He was glad to see D.H. had his beard on. That T.S. had gotten out of the bank.

Now things began to pop. The first bull came into the arena and you never heard such hollering. Ernest was hip to it all, enjoying every minute.

Gertrude said she wanted a Coca-Cola. There was something so American about Gertrude.

"Not now," Ernest said.

"But I want it now," Gertrude said.

Ernest had to get up and go down under the stands to try to find a Coca-Cola. It wasn't easy. Ernest didn't know the Spanish for Coca-Cola. He got a root beer instead. It was the closest thing.

When Ernest came back up in the stands, they were carrying the first bull off. Ernest had missed it.

It was a big crowd and Ernest fought his way along. He had to be careful of his head and nose as well as the root beer.

It was a hard fight but Ernest got to the seats safely. Gertrude's root beer hadn't spilled. But Gertrude was nowhere to be seen.

Kidnapped

At first Ernest wasn't too worried about Gertrude. He thought she might have gone to wash her hands.

Ernest sat down and looked about. Picadors were coming and going. Troubadours were turning somersaults.

Ernest stood up and looked about the stands. He saw D.H. and T.S. and the women. They were waving little pennants. Probably encouraging the bull, Ernest thought. But Gertrude wasn't with them. He didn't see hide nor hair of Gertrude.

He sat down again with the root beer. It was making him all sticky. He wished Gertrude would hurry up. He didn't think her hands were that dirty.

Then there was a big fanfare in the arena, trumpets blowing and picadors shouting. Troubadours and matadors turned hand-springs and jumped about. Ernest expected the bull any moment.

But there was no bull. Instead there was a person with horns. Matadors and troubadours poked and tormented the person with horns.

"I can't believe my eyes," said Ernest.

He looked again and he believed his eyes. It was Gertrude. He could tell by her embroidered necktie. Her horns had slipped to one side.

"Golly day," said Ernest.

He put down the root beer and stepped swiftly across the aisle. He jumped over the fence and onto the field. He ran to Gertrude's side.

"Look here," he said to the picadors, "you can't do that."

He started throwing punches right and left at the picadors. Shortly they were all stretched out on the ground. Unconscious.

Ernest stepped over to Gertrude and snatched the horns from her head.

"Thank you," said Gertrude. She wept she was so humiliated.

Ernest saw Gertrude was badly shaken. He thought he might carry her to the stands. He picked her up and went a few steps. He had to put her down. They walked the rest of the way.

"I'm eternally grateful," Gertrude said, wiping the tears from her eyes.

"Think nothing of it," Ernest said.

When they got to their seats, someone had stolen Gertrude's root beer.

"Six men came up and kidnapped me," Gertrude said, "while you were gone for the Coca-Cola."

"I got you a root beer," Ernest said, "but somebody stole it."

"Six men," said Gertrude.

"Who were they?" Ernest said, looking around suspiciously.

Gertrude only shook her head. "I'm eternally grateful to you for rescuing me. I'd cut off my ear for you."

"Not here," said Ernest.

Bulls came and went all afternoon.

"I'm enjoying it to the hilt," Ernest said, patting Gertrude's hand.

"Yes," said Gertrude. "But it's so unfair. They ought to let the bull carry a spear."

After the last fight, there was a ceremony. Ernest was surprised to find that he was in it.

Two matadors marched up and stood before Ernest, bowing

to him. They acted like he was a big cheese. Ernest got to his feet and Gertrude stood beside him.

One matador read from a scroll. In Spanish, of course. Ernest didn't know what it was all about. The other matador had something on a pillow.

When the one matador stopped reading, the other stepped up with the pillow. He presented Ernest the pillow with a bull's tail on it.

But Ernest wouldn't take it.

"No," said Ernest, shaking his head. "I cannot take it. It won't fit in the icebox at the hotel."

Lovers' Quarrel

After the bullfight, Gertrude and Ernest decided to stroll to the hotel instead of hopping a trolley. The weather was fine, not as fine as Paris, but fine.

"The rain is mostly on the plain," said Gertrude.

"It is, is it?" asked Ernest.

Strolling along, they passed a little shop. Something in the window took Ernest's eye.

"Wait here a moment," Ernest said and went inside.

In a few minutes he was out again with a small, neatly tied package. Ernest gave it to Gertrude.

"For you, Gertrude," Ernest said, "so you will remember Spain."

"Thank you," said Gertrude, "I shall never forget it."

Gertrude opened the package excitedly. Then she saw what it was. "Castanets!" she exclaimed.

"Only they aren't real castanets," Ernest told her. "They're salt and pepper shakers."

"Very nice," said Gertrude. She put them in her pocket quickly.

They strolled further and bumped into Donald Ogden Stewart and Harold Loeb. They were old friends of Ernest's. He introduced them to Gertrude.

Both Donald and Harold gasped. "Gertrude Stein!" they said.

"No less," said Gertrude.

They went on their way and Ernest told Gertrude about Donald and Harold.

"They are fine people," Ernest said. "I might put them in a book sometime.

Then Ernest stopped and bought a paper at a kiosk.

"I like kiosks," Ernest told Gertrude. "They didn't have them up in Michigan."

Now they were at the hotel and had dinner there.

"Bring us anything but an old Spanish custom," Ernest told the waitress. "And plenty of wine."

The waitress came with apple pie and cheese again. But there was plenty of wine. She put wine bottles all over the table.

"That's what I call plenty to eat," said Ernest.

Gertrude had to help him up to the room.

"Don't take my elbow," Ernest said.

Gertrude didn't say anything but took his elbow.

As soon as they got inside the room, Gertrude had a thought.

"I think you'd better walk Basket," Gertrude told Ernest. "And F. Puss too, while you're about it. It's not a bad idea."

"It's not a good idea either," Ernest said. "I haven't read the sports page yet."

"You can't read the sports page," Gertrude told him. "You don't understand Spanish."

Ernest put Basket and F. Puss in their carriers and walked out of the room with them. Gertrude went to the balcony and watched Ernest go down the street with a carrier in either hand.

"Stupid," said Gertrude when Ernest came back, still carrying the carriers, "you're supposed to let the dog and cat walk. Not carry them."

"If you're so smart," said Ernest, "why don't you do it yourself?"

It was their first lovers' quarrel.

The Linen Duster

Now Spain was all but over for Gertrude and Ernest. They must wend their way back to Paris in the Stutz.

"It was a lovely time," Gertrude said.

"Very nice," Ernest said.

They were spending the last hour in the hotel. They had put F. Puss and Basket into the carriers.

"I wonder if they enjoyed the trip," Ernest said.

"I think I'll take off my pants suit," Gertrude said, "and put on my linen duster. It's cooler for traveling."

Gertrude took off her pants suit and put on her linen duster with nothing beneath it.

"It really is cool," said Gertrude.

"You're cool," said Ernest and kissed her.

"Bring me my rose," said Gertrude. Ernest took the rose from the glass and gave it to Gertrude.

"I will keep it forever," Gertrude said.

Now they must leave. Ernest put F. Puss and Basket and the luggage into the Stutz. Ernest checked the tires, got in and pulled his goggles down. They were set to go.

"Wait a minute," said Gertrude. She took a small vase from

the pocket of her linen duster. She'd bought it in a Spanish ten-cent store.

The vase had a little suction cup on it. Gertrude stuck the cup on the windshield. She put her rose in the vase. It worked like magic.

"You are magic, Gertrude," Ernest said. Then they were off.

"One rose," said Gertrude. "I wish for three more."

Ernest wondered what she meant. But now he gave full attention to the Stutz. He hoped there wouldn't be too many flats.

They had gone a way and Ernest stopped the machine. He kissed Gertrude.

"Gertrude," he said.

"Ernest," she said.

It was most charming.

Of course there were flats. Gertrude was a great help to Ernest. Indispensable.

Between the kissing and the flats, there were a number of stops.

"I like the kissing better than the flats," Gertrude said. "Then I don't have to get out of the machine."

"Oh, go on," said Ernest.

And there was yet another flat.

Ernest got out and changed the tire as Gertrude raised an end. Gertrude stood beside Ernest as he finished the task. He gave the wheel a spin.

Somehow Gertrude's linen duster caught in the wheel. It whipped the linen duster right off Gertrude.

"Gertrude!" Ernest said.

"Yes?" said Gertrude.

It was a good thing a machine wasn't passing.

Ernest hurried Gertrude up the road to beat the band. He was heading for a billboard. He got Gertrude behind the billboard just as a machine passed.

"That was close," Ernest said.

The grass behind the billboard was very tall.

"You wait here," said Ernest, "I'll get your pants suit from the machine."

"Please hurry," Gertrude said. "The grass tickles."

Ernest got the pants suit and hastened back.

"Oh, Ernest," Gertrude said. She put her arms around him.

"Put your clothes on," said Ernest.

Gertrude got into the pants suit and they went back to the machine. The linen duster was on the road. Ernest picked it up and put it on the back seat. Basket and F. Puss barked and meowed.

The rest of the trip to Paris was charming. Not too many stops for flats and more for kissing.

"It's all so charming," Gertrude said.

"April in Paris," said Ernest.

"It's July," Gertrude told him.

"Chestnuts in blossom," Ernest said.

"That old chestnut," said Gertrude.

Then they were home. Gertrude was home.

"27 rue de Fleurus," Gertrude said.

"Sounds familiar," Ernest said.

Alice had left a light in the upstairs window. The ladder was still up.

"Darling," said Gertrude.

Ernest kissed her hand and then her lips. Very quickly, very lightly. Alice might be watching.

Ernest took Basket and the suitcase from the machine. Gertrude got out.

It was a fine moonlight night. Ernest didn't need to flash his flashlight.

Ernest steadied the ladder and Gertrude took Basket up. She came down for the suitcase.

"And my rose," said Gertrude. "My rose. I must have my rose." She went to the Stutz and took the rose and the vase too.

"It was roses, roses all the way," said Ernest.

It was parting time. Quickly, roughly they kissed.

"Be careful of my nose," Ernest said.

"I'm sorry," said Gertrude.

She went in her purse, took out a latch key and pressed it into Ernest's hand. "Here," Gertrude said. "For you."

She went up with the suitcase and got in the window. She turned and blew a kiss to Ernest.

Ernest blew one back. Then he turned the Stutz around, honked once, and was on his way to the sawmill.

BETWEEN THE ACTS

Cinematically Speaking

Reader, shall we speak of things cinematic?

After all the high drama lately, a little chat might help.

May we inquire, reader, do you go to the cinema?

Ah, the cinema. Though we cherish it, we do not think it is ready for our little volume.

Let us speak of bare bodies.

At last count there were six in our volume. We do not promise more. On the other hand, one might pop up at any moment.

We know full well the cinema of late has been fraught with bare bodies.

And you, no doubt, have viewed some of them. But, tell us, reader, how did the cinema handle their bodies? Not too well, we think.

If we do say so ourself, we believe we have handled our bare bodies with finesse.

Consider in our work, if you will, the party scene. Here there was music and dancing. Songs were sung, we believe. A kind of joyfulness prevailed, even, we might say, innocence.

The women on the pedestals were all mothers, we believe. They had Bumby. What are clothes to mothers? What are bare bodies? Further, they were poor and had no bathing garments to wear.

The woman who danced on the little table was also a mother. And more than that, she was expressing her individuality. In a delightful way, we thought.

And later in our work, there was the roadside and billboard scene. We tried to handle it in very good taste. The woman may not have been a mother but she was mature.

And further, it was an accident. There was nothing premeditated about it. A wheel turned, a bit of cloth caught and a garment was torn away. It could have happened to anyone who wore a linen duster with nothing beneath it.

No, we do not think the cinema is ready for us.

And, if it were, there is the matter of casting.

Take the heroine. Perhaps Vanessa Redgrave might do. If her father would let her. Perhaps Mary Miles Minter or Blanche Sweet.

There is always Margaret Dumont or maybe one of the Hepburn sisters. But Margaret Rutherford is our first choice. Claudette Colbert our second.

And the hero, likewise, presents difficulties.

Someone from the silent films would do very well. William S. Hart or Charles "Buck" Jones. Then there is Ben Blue. Or perhaps Sessue Hayakawa.

But we must stand up for Woody Allen. We think he is immeasurably capable. But he is writing for *The New Republic* nowadays. Or *The Kenyon Review.*

Rutherford and Allen would be an endearing team.

We are sorry to have taken so much of your time, reader. But the cinema does interest us. We thought it might interest you too.

Now, as they say, on with the story.

ACT FOUR

An Understanding

What can we say about things back at the sawmill?

Back at the sawmill, things had been hell for three days. That is how long it has been since Ernest returned.

For three days the wives had been trying to get out of Ernest where he had been.

But Ernest was his usual taciturn self like his prose. He didn't give an inch. He knew they would take a mile. He said nothing.

"What's the matter," Pauline said, "the cat got your tongue?"

"You'd know more about cats," Ernest said, "if you took care of F. Puss."

F. Puss was a bone of contention as usual.

"How come a cat has a carrier and I don't have a bathing suit?" Martha asked.

"Maybe the cat deserves it more," said Ernest.

That was the way it went on, one thing after another.

"Why don't you start the dusting rigmarole?" said Ernest.

They started the dusting rigmarole. "That's what I get for asking," Ernest said.

"What's all this horns and tomato business?" Mary said.

"I'll tell you what it is," Ernest said. "None of your business."

119

And all the wives were tired of Ernest's bandages. The horns and tomato were long gone, replaced by white cloth, but they wouldn't let Ernest forget.

One after the other would ask, "How about the horns and tomato business?"

And they wanted to know when he was going to give up on the bandaging. They were tired to death of it.

"There's nothing the matter with your nose," Mary said. "And nothing more than usual the matter with your head."

Was it any wonder Ernest put F. Puss in the carrier and stalked out of the sawmill?

Ernest remembered about Gertrude. How she didn't like it when he carried Basket and F. Puss down the street.

Maybe Gertrude was right. But putting a cat in a carrier was a convenient way of walking it. Ernest thought Alice might do the same thing with Basket. When Gertrude wasn't looking, of course.

Ernest was thinking more and more of Gertrude. He thought of how he'd thrown her the rose when the bull was after him. He thought of how she changed the water in the glass every ten minutes. And what did she mean about three more roses? She had said something about three more roses.

Then Ernest got it in a flash. He thought how dull he had been not to understand. Gertrude had one rose and wanted three more. One plus three is four. Four roses. It was that simple.

Four Roses in Three Acts. It was Gertrude's opera. Virgil had written it for her.

Ernest wondered how he had been so blind. How could he not have understood? Of course Gertrude wanted three more roses. So there'd be four roses. Ernest would make it up to her somehow. He had been blind, blind.

Ezra And The Chair

And the last three days at 27 rue de Fleurus, they weren't so peachy either. Since Gertrude had climbed up the ladder to get home.

"I never want to see another dish," said Alice.

"What would you eat from?" asked Gertrude.

It was the old dishes business, going round and round.

"And dusting," Gertrude said. "Did you dust while I was away?"

"I let Basket do it," Alice said. Alice was taking another dig at Gertrude for taking Basket with her.

"And have you walked Basket?" asked Gertrude.

"No," said Alice. "And I haven't put the ladder away either. Or would you like it there permanently?"

Gertrude just didn't answer. Maybe she'd learned a thing or two from Ernest.

"And the rose business," said Alice. "What's the rose business? Changing the water every ten minutes."

It was Ernest's rose, of course. The one he had tossed to Gertrude.

"I like roses," Gertrude said noncommittally. It was true. Gertrude did like roses.

Dishes, dusting, ladders, Basket, roses. It went on and on.

And then Ezra Pound dropped by. He and Gertrude talked of literature and life. He didn't bring his wife with him. Alice was furious.

"Who am I to sit with?" Alice asked Gertrude.

"Oh, sit down," said Gertrude.

Ezra Pound was standing and he thought Gertrude was talking to him. Ezra sat down and rather hard. Ezra sometimes did things the hard way.

But the trouble was, it was Gertrude's favorite chair. William James had given it to her at Radcliffe. The college had given William James a chair, so he occasionally gave one to other people.

Ezra crashed to the floor, smashing Gertrude's favorite chair.

Gertrude was greatly shaken. She called Alice to help Ezra up. But first Alice had to help Gertrude up. Out of her chair, that is. Sometimes Gertrude would get stuck in her chair.

Gertrude went over and examined the damaged chair.

"Get me up," Ezra shouted. "Get me out of here." He was tangled in the broken chair. Alice was trying to get him up.

"You broke my favorite chair," Gertrude said somewhat sorely to Ezra.

"I'll break your head," Ezra shouted.

Somehow Ezra did get up. And he headed straight for the door.

"And don't come back," Gertrude said. "Breaking my favorite chair."

It was not a very nice way for Gertrude to end a conversation on life and literature with Ezra Pound. But we shall forgive her, won't we? Partly.

That was Gertrude. Gertrude was edgy. Gertrude was pining. Gertrude was pining for Ernest.

Four Roses

Ernest went to the best florist in Paris.

"I want some roses," Ernest said. "Long-stemmed ones, please. Four of them."

The shopkeeper brought forth some long-stemmed roses.

"Not long enough," said Ernest. "And make them red."

The shopkeeper brought some long long-stemmed red ones. The stems reached from Ernest's knees to his nose.

"That's the ticket," said Ernest. "Wrap them, please."

"Of course I'll wrap them," the shopkeeper said. "What kind of a shop do you think this is?"

Ernest carried the roses out before him. He was going to 27 rue de Fleurus.

Ernest was without wheels. The Stutz was in the garage for repairs. As usual. It was something with the valves. Or was it the brakes? He hoped they wouldn't remove the bumper sticker.

Ernest had seen a new bumper sticker he wanted to get. It said:

SWEEP THE SIDEWALKS WITH AL

Ernest wondered who Al was.

Besides the roses, Ernest carried Gertrude's linen duster. She had left it behind in the Stutz.

Ernest could see Gertrude standing beside the Stutz now without her linen duster.

Ernest had had the linen duster cleaned and pressed. And scented.

Ernest heard that they scented things in Paris. He had the thing scented.

Ernest was there now. He saw the ladder still beside the window. For a brief moment Ernest thought he might run up it. Then he thought he'd better not. Something else might happen to him.

And he had the latch key, didn't he? Gertrude's latch key.* He thought how she had pressed his hand. "Here," she said. "For you." Then she ran up the ladder.

But he wasn't going to run up the ladder.

Then another thought struck Ernest. He was thinking all the time now.

Suppose I let myself in with the latch key, Ernest thought. Surprise Gertrude. Surprise Gertrude with the roses, Ernest thought.

Ernest took the latch key and quietly turned it and quietly let himself into 27 rue de Fleurus.

---

*We hope, dear reader, you have not forgotten the latch key. We have not.

Something Of His Heart

It was all quiet inside 27 rue de Fleurus, at least as far as Ernest could tell. He went into the big picture room. The pictures seemed bigger to Ernest than ever. And more of them.

"Gertrude sure has a lot of pictures," Ernest said to himself.

Ernest sat down and looked at some of the pictures. There was one of a woman without any clothes that was blue. Ernest wondered why the woman was blue. Well, women sometimes are blue in Paris, Ernest thought.

Ernest sat very straight in his chair looking at the pictures. Ernest himself was a picture. An etching by Norman Rockwell. He had the flowers out before him in one hand, the linen duster in the other.

No, we are wrong. Ernest was not a Norman Rockwell etching. He was Norman Rockwell himself.*

Then Ernest heard voices. From out of the kitchen or somewheres. Sure enough it was Gertrude. She was talking to someone. Yes, it was Alice.

"I'm tired of dusting," Alice said. "All I ever do is dust."

"How about when you do the dishes?" Gertrude said.

"That's even worse," Alice said. "Dusting and doing dishes,

125

dusting and doing dishes, dusting and doing dishes. That's all I ever do." Alice was crying now.

"That's not so," said Gertrude. "I let you put the ladder up, didn't I?"

"It was because you wanted to get down," Alice said.

Ernest was very quiet, taking it all in.

It was more interesting than the pictures. Gertrude and Alice didn't know he was there.

"You don't do dusting," Alice told Gertrude.

"Now Alice," said Gertrude.

"You don't do dishes," Alice said.

"You know I can't stand on my feet," Gertrude said.

"How else would you stand?" Alice asked. "You don't walk Basket."

"Now Alice," Gertrude said, "you know you need the exercise."

The voices were coming out of the kitchen or somewheres.

"It sounds almost like home to me," said Ernest to himself. "My own little sawmill."

Then suddenly Ernest saw it all in a different light.

It was true. It was true. Alice did dust, do the dishes, walk Basket and all the rest of it.

Ernest heard Alice crying hard now in the kitchen or somewheres.

Ernest thought of Pamplona. Why, in Pamplona, he, Ernest, had to walk Basket, didn't he? And then Gertrude said he walked him the wrong way, didn't she?

Suddenly Ernest had a vision of himself walking Basket. Walking Basket all his life. In a carrier or not, didn't make any difference.

Then he saw himself washing dishes.

It was so sad, so sad about Alice, Ernest thought. But what could he do? What could he do? Ernest could stand it no longer.

Ernest got up from the chair, hoping it wouldn't creak. He stepped to the table and put the linen duster on it. He took the latch key from his pocket and placed it beside the linen duster.

Ernest looked toward where the voices were coming. From the kitchen or somewheres. The voices had come and he had heard. They did not know he had heard.

"Good-bye," said Ernest softly.

Ernest went quickly to the door, taking the roses with him. Quietly Ernest let himself out of 27 rue de Fleurus.

But Ernest left something there other than the linen duster. Other than the latch key. Ernest left something of his heart there at 27 rue de Fleurus.

---

*It is not known if Norman Rockwell were in Paris at this time. He might have been.

Lovely As Roses

When the wives saw Ernest returning to the sawmill, a strange thing happened. The wives at first didn't know it was Ernest, didn't recognize him. Not a wife recognized Ernest.

On his way home, Ernest had removed his head and nose bandages. He had had enough of them. He felt like a new man.

No wonder his wives didn't recognize him.

And then too, he carried roses. No wife had ever seen Ernest carry roses before.

Ernest burst in through the sawmill door. Now the wives recognized him. He had no bandages, he had roses.

The wives greeted Ernest with smiles. Ernest's smile was wider than all the wives' smiles put together.

"How are my wives?" said Ernest. "You are all lovely, lovely as roses."

It was so. They were all lovely as roses. Ernest saying it was so, made it doubly so.

Then Ernest presented each wife a rose.

"Four roses you are," he said. "Each of you a rose."

And Ernest played with Bumby. Ernest tried to ride the hobby horse. Broke it, of course. Then Ernest had to go out and buy a new one.

At 27 rue de Fleurus, the picture was not as joyous.

Gertrude had found the linen duster and latch key. Or, rather, Alice had found them and taken them to Gertrude. Gertrude seldom found anything.

Gertrude wept a bit. Alice consoled her.

Gertrude had her rose. The one rose from Ernest. She went and changed the water. She would never have four roses.

Alice took the ladder down for good.

And life went on at 27 rue de Fleurus. And literature. Gertrude wrote and wrote. And Alice did the dishes.

Gertrude in Pamplona. Ernest in Pamplona. Gertrude and Ernest in Pamplona. Gertrude in Paris. Ernest in Paris. Gertrude and Ernest in Paris. Let this be their epitaph:

Theirs was a love that wasn't.

AFTER THE ACTS

Paris Never Ends

There is never any end to Paris. There is never any beginning to it either. Paris runs in circles. Especially at the Place Vendôme.
Everyone brings something to Paris. Everyone takes something away. Usually less money.
Sometimes one brings one wife and takes away another. Sometimes two couples come and switch.
Some say Paris is for the young and poor. Some say Paris is for the old and rich. Take your choice.
Some lovers quarrel and others make up. Others go without any make-up at all.
Everyone says you should go to Paris to die. Everyone comes away half dead.
One day you pick up the flowers from a flower girl. One night you pick up the flower girl.
Paris is joy and sorrow and you cannot tell the difference. Paris is laughter and tears and you can tell the difference. Tears are wet.
You walk along the Seine and it is lovely. Another time you want to jump in.
You sit in a café and never want to leave. Especially if you have

no money. Then you wash the café dishes.

They may tear down Les Halles but there is always Le Supermarché.

You may cringe at a toy Eiffel Tower because it isn't the real thing.

And in the Luxembourg Gardens, the flowers come again each spring. Each spring.

Paris is the endless rose that blooms again each spring.

But Forgive Us

So, reader, we thank you again. And for the last time. You have been a good reader. You have stayed with us to the end.

We truly hope you have not been disappointed with our story. Or with its ending. Was the ending as you expected? There was some sadness in it, don't you think? And surely some gladness too. That is the way life is.

Somehow we thought there was so much to say here. Now we feel strangely quiet. Maybe because now it is your turn to talk. Go ahead, talk, good reader.

Say what you will, but forgive us.

May Gertrude and Ernest smile. But if they do not smile, may they too forgive us. Gertrude and Ernest in heaven. Heaven is where all good writers go.

And now, good reader, good-bye.

Würzburg
Heigenbrücken
Paris
Neuchâtel
Frankfurt
Baltimore

About the Author:

The author has actually been in Paris and Pamplona but spends most of his time in Baltimore with his wife, cat, and lots of books. He once worked on the *Sunpapers* (shades of H.L.Mencken) where he was, he thinks, a copy editor. But he gave it up for the good life. He is at last a writer only, or didn't Scott Fitzgerald say that?

Asked for an estimate of his own work, the author replied: "Possibly the finest of our time. John Barth, Samuel Beckett, Henny Youngman must move over." This is his short estimate. Do not ask him for a long one.

FICTION COLLECTIVE
Books in Print:

The Second Story Man by Mimi Albert
Althea by J.M.Alonso
Searching for Survivors by Russell Banks
Babble by Jonathan Baumbach
Reruns by Jonathan Baumbach
Things in Place by Jerry Bumpus
Ø *Null Set* by George Chambers
Amateur People by Andrée Connors
Take It or Leave It by Raymond Federman
Museum by B.H.Friedman
Temporary Sanity by Thomas Glynn
The Talking Room by Marianne Hauser
Holy Smoke by Fanny Howe
Mole's Pity by Harold Jaffe
Moving Parts by Steve Katz
Find Him! by Elaine Kraf
Emergency Exit by Clarence Major
Four Roses in Three Acts by Franklin Mason
The Secret Table by Mark Mirsky
Encores for a Dilettante by Ursule Molinaro
Rope Dances by David Porush
The Broad Back of the Angel by Leon Rooke
The Comatose Kids by Seymour Simckes
Fat People by Carol Sturm Smith
The Hermetic Whore by Peter Spielberg
Twiddledum Twaddledum by Peter Spielberg
Long Talking Bad Conditions Blues by Ronald Sukenick
98.6 by Ronald Sukenick
Meningitis by Yuriy Tarnawsky
Heretical Songs by Curtis White
Statements 1
Statements 2